Sex, Dead Dogs, and Me The Paperback!

Ed Williams

Sex, Dead Dogs, and Me
The Paperback!

Ed Williams

Southern Charm Press
Hampton, Georgia
1-888-281-9393
www.southerncharmpress.com

This book is based on the author's recollection and perception of events. Because the object of this book is to entertain instead of inform, the author has taken liberty and let his imagination alter all the events and characters described in this book. In particular, names, places, and dates were altered to avoid embarrassing anyone.

Copyright © 2000 by Ed Williams
All rights reserved.Southern Charm Press,
150 Caldwell Drive, Hampton, GA 30228
Visit our Web site at www.southerncharmpress.com

The publisher offers discounts on this book when purchased in
quantities. For more information, contact:
toll free: 1-888-281-9393, phone: 770-946-5211, fax: 770-946-5220,
e-mail: info@southerncharmpress.com

Printed in the United States of America
First Printing: December 2000

Library of Congress Card Number
LCCN 00-192128

Williams, Ed
Sex, Dead Dogs, and Me –The Paperback! / Ed Williams
ISBN 0-9702190-1-6

Illustration design by Brooks Dantzler

Photography by Jim Messer

FOREWORD

I guess any damn thing can happen, can't it?

I mean it. Over the past year or so, I've had some of the damndest experiences of my life, all caused because of writing down these stories about Juliette. I've met BTO, been the prototype for the lead male character in a romance novel, discovered ten times over what book groupies are, and now I'm about to see this book go out again as a paperback. Who would've ever thought it?

The best analogy I can give re all this is to imagine yourself in the backyard, scratching your butt. As you enjoy the blessed relief, someone slips up behind you and says, "Hey, with that arm motion, you should be pitching for the New York Yankees! Here's a million dollar contract!" That's what writing has been for me, an ass scratching that has resulted in a little bit of money and a whole lot of very interesting experiences.

That all being said, let's take a trip back to Juliette, Georgia, a place where the living is special, the laughs are genuine, and the women always make you smile.

ACKNOWLEDGMENTS

There are lots of people I need to thank for making "Sex, Dead Dogs, and Me - The Paperback!" possible:

To Ed Jr., the best father and life's advisor there is. I've put him through a lot of hassle on account of this book, which makes me appreciate him all the more.

To Alison and Will, the two best yard apes a dad could ever be blessed with.

To the Brotherhood, Ray and Hugh - thanks for letting me tell the world about all that stuff we did, even though the three of us know there's still a lot left unsaid.

To Rebecca Paisley, Kelly Milner-Halls, and Linda Bleser - ya'll will never know how much the early encouragement you gave me meant, and because of the three of you I'm still sitting here today writing these crazy damn stories.

To BTO, the best damn band in the world.

To Keith Giddeon, the People's Webmaster, for working all the magic with our webpage.

To Brooks Danzler, who did the cover art for this book, and holds the cherished title of "Artist to the Brotherhood."

To Terry Bellflower, who bought the first hardback copy of "Sex, Dead Dogs, and Me", and to whom I'm giving a copy of the first paperback. Book collectors, this is the man you want to talk to if these damn books sell.

To the following friends, who helped me in one way or the other, and who all deserve honorary Brotherhood memberships: Dr. Boland, Cliff Chandler, Geri Teran, Jackie K. Cooper, Diane Crosby, David Evans, Ed Grisamore, Jeannie Hogue, Rebecca Taylor, Charlie

Lanphier, Sheri Martin, Alex Gregory, David Meade, Sandra Okamoto, Joy Padgett, Todd Smith, Glenda Beall, Katherine Turk, Jennifer Sinclair, Rusty Trice, Billy Yarbrough, Rob Gibson, and Kelli Toler.

And finally, to Kathy Williams, my publisher and good friend who is the real reason for all the writing related stuff I'm doing these days. I'd smooch her if it wouldn't get me into a helluva lot of trouble.

Table of Contents

CHAPTER 1

SEX, DEAD DOGS, AND ME

God, I wish I was seventeen again.....

No, I'm not about to write some flowery literary prose about the wonders of being young. Nor am I going to wax poetic on the trials and tribulations of youthfulness.

The best thing, I think, about being young is the focus it brings to one's life. That may come off as a bit odd, seeing as how most people look at youth as being a very disorienting time. I didn't find this to be true at all - I found genuine focus in my teenage years.

It really does make some sense. Let me be clearer - as I'm writing this, I'm forty years old. Born and raised in Juliette, Georgia (where the movie "Fried Green Tomatoes" was filmed), I'm married and have two children. Been married sixteen years and the kids (Alison and Will) are thirteen and ten. I hold a position as Human Resources Director for two companies, attend church pretty regularly, etc, etc.

If you consider all that, its easy to see that I can't have much focus in my life now. Everything seems to be a damn blur that shuffles between the raising of my kids, work responsibilities, marriage, etc. Sometimes I honestly don't know what I'm supposed to be doing or where I'm supposed to be at any particular point in the day. It's a problem all we middle-aged, middle-class, yogurt-sucking yuppies face.

Ahhhh, but the teen years - they were different. The teen years provided true focus for me. I knew then what the most important thing in life was. Whatever I was doing - attending school, being at home, going to church, or whatever - the most important thing to me in life was sex.

And why not? At seventeen my youthful body was pumping hormones like a Jerry Lee Lewis piano. I loved it, too. There was nothing better than seeing a nice looking young lady and letting your mind and salivary glands froth with unbridled excitement. I can remember one time pulling a woodie so hard in a tenth grade history class that it pushed my shorts into my zipper and hung them up. When I went to the bathroom to try to extricate them, I tore the front of my underwear up as I unzipped my fly. It took me several minutes of serious work before I could get my shorts freed from my zipper. Once freed, I could allow the pink crusader to get out of its confinement and release a Lake Michigan sized urination that I had been holding back.

The need for sex was worse for me than most because of growing up in a rural area like Juliette. My parents (Ed Jr. and Barbra) lived in a house that literally sat between a cow pasture and a pond. Until I hit sixteen and got my driver's license, my social life was no more than the things I did at school, home, or church.

Then everything changed. Now I could get out of Juliette and begin to sample a little more of what life had to offer.

I entered my senior year of high school going steady with a girl named Jenny. Jenny was very cute and I liked her a lot. She was also intelligent and was even taking some college classes in addition to her high school classes. We were pretty close even though we did spar a little at times - Jenny was very independent and I don't tend to be a shrinking violet, so, we did bump heads from time to time.

The only problem with my relationship with Jenny was that she was a nice girl. A very nice girl. She was the kinda girl you wanted to marry, but, I went home many nights after seeing her so hard that I would wonder if I had concrete running through my bloodstream. If anything, Jenny made my sexual urges even stronger than they had been before. For a teenage boy, this had its good and bad points. It was good to want to have sex but it was frustrating not to be able to. (Frustrating isn't really the word I want to use here but the appropriate cuss words would get me in trouble).

As we got into our senior year at Mary Persons High, I occupied a lot of my time by playing football. Playing football for Mary Persons was the ultimate athletic thing you could do. The football team regularly drew five to six thousand people to its games in a county where the population was five to six thousand. Those of us that played football were treated like little gods. We could leave classes, get free food and stuff from various merchants, and one service station even washed our cars for free. And the girls......

What I mean here is that I was starting to get a little attention from some of the other girls at school besides Jenny. Guys on the team would tell me about this girl or that girl liking me. I would always be totally amazed at this. Then (and now) I have a hard time imagining any woman being attracted to me. Basically, I'm average looking and have average intelligence. But damned if there weren't some high school girls who had designs on me. And inside, I was wrestling the age old internal struggle between good and evil - should I stay true to Jenny and suffer from swollen groinitis, or, should I sin and go after other women?

It wasn't even close - sinning won. I decided to see what some of these other girls had to offer. Had no moral problems about it, either - see, I told you I was focused. And to be focused you have to be sure about what you're doing. I was damn sure about what I wanted to do.

I started dating a whole lot. So much so that Ed Jr. told me to not feel like "you have to hone every tulip in Monroe County." I guess that he was concerned that I was burning the candle too brightly at both ends. But, I sure did like getting out and having fun, and my "candle" was having a good time as well.

Seems like it was the early part of 1974 when a relationship started that caused me to understand the real power of the attraction to the opposite sex. I was walking to class one day and talking with my good friend Ray Pippin (one-third of the Brotherhood, the most elite social organization in the world). Ray mentioned to me that he had heard a rumour about a young lady liking me.

Of course, I asked the Pip immediately who this girl was. He said, "Mary, Mary Jenkins. I hear she talks about you a lot and for some reason wants to see your sorry ass." I asked Ray if he was sure about this? He informed me that he was not a psychic but that he had gotten it from a pretty reliable source.

This started me thinking. Mary went to the same church Jenny did. I had even met and talked to her there a couple of times. She had long, blond hair and was prettier than hell. The rest of her wasn't too badly designed, either.

I was smiling to myself thinking about how much fun it would be to see her. This daydream was goin' pretty good until the Pip said, "Well, no way in hell you can date her with her goin' to Jenny's church and all."

I took that remark as a challenge - just why couldn't I date her? I wasn't married and Jenny was so damn independent. She'd say stuff like, "We're just seeing each other, Edward. I am still my own woman." I figured that was fine but that it also meant that she wasn't going to seriously commit to me. As I thought more about all this, the better I was feeling about starting a relationship with Marcy.

The next step in my plan was to somehow get a date with Mary. As I rode to school on the bus a few days later someone mentioned that the "Elvis - Aloha From Hawaii" TV special was going to be on television that upcoming Friday night. I am a huge Elvis fan. With me, musically, there is Elvis and a second tier of Bachman-Turner Overdrive (the best damn band in the world), The Guess Who, Buddy Holly, Jerry Lee Lewis, Atlanta Rhythm Section, and Gordon Lightfoot. After them, everyone else is dwelling in murky musical depths somewhere far below.

It hit me that if I watched Elvis at home that I would have to watch it on our black and white TV. Color TV was popular and I was dying to see the King in his full splendor. As I mulled this over the thought occurred to me that Mary might have a color TV. If she did, and I could somehow get invited over to her house to watch it, I could see both her and Elvis.

What a damn good plan - made perfect sense to me! As I got to school that morning, I kept my eyes peeled for Mary in the hallway. Sure enough, right after lunch, I saw Mary walk by in the opposite direction headed to her math class or something. As she walked by I said, "Mary?"

Mary stopped, looked at me, and smiled "Yes?"

"Do you have a color TV?"

Mary replied that she did.

I said, "Well, if you're smart you'll invite me over Friday night to watch Elvis with you."

Mary smiled really big and said that that was fine with her. I told her that I'd be at her house around seven and that I looked forward to it. She gave me another nice smile - one that I still remember now.

I walked away from her feeling like the coolest dude alive. Two women! And the funny thing was, I wasn't trying to keep it a secret or anything. I remember thinking that I must have been a Valentino-in-training. The man - a veritable Ric Flair, Joe Namath, and Hugh Hefner all rolled into one.

That week couldn't pass by fast enough for me. Finally, Friday did roll around. I was impatient as hell all day, and it didn't help that I had seen Mary a couple of times in the hallway. She had flashed that nice smile of hers and even checked to make sure that I was going to be over that evening. Somehow I got through the day, hopped on the school bus, and made my way home.

Once at the house I made damn sure that I took a shower and put on my coolest clothes. I even shaved again, as with black hair one's beard shows up pretty distinctly after a whole day at school. I then slapped on a little of Ed Jr.s' Old Spice, which is something I had never done before. There was no doubt that I was looking forward, in a big way, to seeing Miss Jenkins.

Around seven I left my house and drove over to Mary's in my souped-up Volkswagen bug. That car was cool - big headlamps, huge tires, dual chrome exhaust pipes, and lots of back seat space (no back seat actually, just a carpeted platform). Since I have no sense of direction, and could end up in Florida on any given trip, I used a map that Mary had drawn for me so that I would be sure to find her house.

As I pulled up in her driveway, it hit me that she lived on the same road that Jenny did. It also dawned on me that Jenny's house was only about a mile up the road. I have to admit I took an almost perverse pleasure in this, but, this situation was destined to have negative consequences for me as you will see later on in this yarn.

I walked to the front door and knocked. Mary's mom Helen answered it. She looked at me and said, "You must be Edward." I smiled and told her I was. She invited me in, asked how my parents were, and motioned me into the den.

Mary was sitting there on the sofa looking very pretty. She had on a nice sweater, and her blonde hair cascaded down around her shoulders. And again she had a beautiful smile. I couldn't stop looking at her, but, I did manage to stumble over to the sofa and sit down with her.

We sat there sort of awkwardly for awhile, engaging in some really peripheral type chit chat. We both knew that we were doing something a little forbidden and, down deep, we both were enjoying it. We talked for awhile and then I noticed that Elvis was gonna be on in about ten minutes.

One bad habit that I have is that I love to drink lots of fluids. Whole lots of em'. By the time I had gotten out of school and over to Mary's house, I had downed five or six cokes. My Pacific Ocean sized bladder was signaling me in an urgent way that it was time to unload its cargo. The only problem was that I had this thing about not wanting to my date to see that I needed to go to the bathroom. It was a crazy quirk, but, for some reason, I thought it made me look less than cool.

Cool is one thing, but when you have to whiz so bad that sweat is beading up on your forehead, it's another. I asked Mary where her bathroom was and she got up and showed me. I casually strolled in there, smiling as I shut the door behind me.

It's true what they say about the simplest pleasures in life being the best. You know, I can still remember how relieved I felt while taking that piss. As I stood there enjoying it, it hit me as to how perfect the male organ really is. Its located pretty much out of the way on a guy's body and it serves two damn important purposes - and, the best thing is, both those purposes are both fun and meaningful.

I got through whizzing and zipped my pants up as quickly as I could - didn't want Mary to note that I was in there very long. The bad thing was, I was trying to get through so fast that I zipped my shorts up in my zipper.

I tried like hell to extricate them but I had zipped them up so fast that they were securely caught in the teeth of that zipper. I wanted to cuss real bad but I knew I dare not at Mary's house. And the clock was ticking - only two more minutes until the King in Concert. I let panic overtake me and I yanked my shirttail out of my pants and let it hang outside. That way, it would cover the expanse of white jockey shorts that was peering out through the teeth of my zipper.

I coolly walked back into the room and sat down with Mary. She stared at me and asked why was my shirttail out? I calmly replied that all the football players did that the first time they went out with a girl (what a crock of shit that was). It was like, a football player's thing and it meant that we liked the girl. At that comment, Mary smiled real big and I figured I was out of the woods on that issue.

The show began and Elvis was really wowing the crowd. I was totally engrossed in the concert, as typically I am with all things Elvis, but, I did chat with Mary a little to be polite. As the concert progressed, I found that I was talking with Mary more and more and was watching the concert less and less. Finally, the inevitable happened - we were sitting close together on that sofa, looking into each other's eyes and....

We smooched - a nice, long wet one. In fact, we kept kissing each other over and over. To be blunt, it was a round of tonsil hockey that I didn't duplicate until I started dating an Atlanta city woman a few years later. Mary and I finally pulled our selves apart, both breathing heavy but trying to look composed. We stammered a few words to each other - I can't even remember what I said to her. I do know we agreed to see each other the following Friday night.

I went home at this point even more convinced that I was the coolest man alive. What made it even better was my date the next night with Jenny. I did find with her that I was a lot more relaxed and didn't seem to care quite as much as to how she felt about things. We had a pretty good date, I went home, and nothing else was very memorable about it.

When I got to school the next Monday I saw Mary. She was smiling at me and asked if Friday night was still on? I told her it sure was. Then she asked me if she could wear my football letter jacket? I didn't even hesitate - I took it off and gave it to her, right there on the spot.

At this point, things got much more itchy as regards my "love triangle". Mary wore that jacket all the time and our relationship then became known all around the school. It lead to some very interesting situations.

First off, Friday night was Mary's and Saturday night was Jenny's. I was starting to be more exhausted on Sunday's than I had been on weekends after football games. The second problem was that both Jenny and Mary knew I was seeing the other. I loved Mary's reaction to it - she wanted to see me, made no bones about it, and wore that jacket all the time. Jenny, on the other hand, was being the mature woman and tried to act as if she didn't really care about me seeing Mary. Down deep I think it was a load of crap but that was how Jenny wanted to respond to the situation.

The third interesting situation occurred when Mary and I went out on our first real date. After seeing each other a few more Fridays, Mary's mom consented to let her go out on a real date with me. We were both really excited about this - we talked a lot about where we would go and what we would do. Finally, we decided that we would go to a romantic movie (Romeo and Juliet, the one with the dark-haired gal - Olivia something - that hung her large dairies out of her Juliet dress) at the Westgate Theatre in Macon.

The night of our date came and I picked Mary up and took her to Macon. We sat up under each other in the theatre and kissed till' our lips looked like pitted prunes. After two and a half hours of that, we struggled out of our seats, got in the car, and began the drive back to Mary's house.

For me to get Mary home I had to drive right by Jenny's house. This is the point where fate stepped in and dealt me a cruel hand. Mary and I were riding along, blissfully unaware of what fate was about to bring. I drove slowly, mainly because the engine on that Volkswagen was loud and I sure didn't want Jenny to hear it. As Mary and I cruised by Jenny's house, Jenny's dog (its name was Barfy or Fluffy or some other damn name like that) ran right in front of my car - it literally came out of nowhere! I didn't even have a chance to hit the brakes! I nailed Fluffy or Barfy with a direct hit - in fact, the hit was so direct that the dog sort of spiraled off to the right like a football into the night.

Mary exclaimed, "We need to get out and check on that dog!" I said,

"Mary, the dog is dead. There is nothing we can do for it!" Mary then replied,

"We should at least let the people that own it know what happened!" I told Mary that I felt like she had lost her mind. Reviving the dead was not our business, and besides, she would be late getting home. Reluctantly, she agreed to go home and I secretly breathed one the greatest sighs of relief that I have ever breathed.

The next day, I decided to phone Jenny around 2 o'clock in the afternoon. We chatted about many different things. After about 20 minutes of small-talk Jenny said, "A terrible thing happened last night." I said, "What?" Jenny said, " Our little dog, Buffy (or Barfy or Muffin or whatever), was hit by a car last night and was killed! What's worse, the person that hit him didn't even bother to stop and tell us what had happened!" To this, I replied in a clear, convincing manner, "There are a lot of mean sonofabitches in this world."

Now, there are some basic lessons that should be learned from this event. If you didn't pick up on these intuitively, this is what they are:

1. If a dog is dead, it's dead. This is indisputable. I had no doubt that upon impact, little Barfy (or Rex or Spot or whatever) was gone. There was nothing that could be done, save pronouncing last rites.

2. There is a balance to be maintained between confession and the consequences of confessing. In this case, it seemed to me that a far greater balance could be maintained by not confessing instead of giving a full confession. Confessing meant that Jenny would be upset, our relationship hurt, maybe ruined forever, and her dog would still be dead. By not confessing, the relationship stayed great but her dog was still dead. Anyway you cut it, the smart thing to do was to stay quiet.

3. For all you animal purists out there that are shocked and offended by this remember one thing- a leash on that dog would have prevented all of this. I even brought this up to Jenny and I am sure that their dogs had leashes on them after this episode. Remember, it took the Titanic sinking for there to be enough lifeboats to carry everyone on a ship in case it went down.

4. The dating game is a cruel and unusual thing. One man's happiness can be one dog's downfall. You never, ever, know.

Mary and I stopped seeing each other soon after this because I was getting tired of dating so much. I also got tired of all the problems associated with dating two people at the same time. I did learn a couple of lessons from this whole episode, though. The first was that you can't use people and not pay a price for it. One of the biggest fears I have now is that if this book ever gets published that Jenny will hear about it, buy one, and then learn that it was me that killed her dog. I can see her stern visage at a book signing somewhere. "Hi mam, want me to sign your book?" "Yes, you filthy dog killing shit!" she replies. Not a real heart warming thought, for sure. That is potential problem number one.

Secondly, being hormonally driven can lead to some bad situations. The worse thing here is that although I initially saw Mary cause I lusted for her, later I came to realize that I genuinely cared about her. When I did realize that, it was too late. I had left her and she wasn't about to come back. Can't say that I blamed her, either. I did get the chance a couple of years later to tell her that I really cared for her and what a fool I'd been. Mary smiled and nodded and I was left to think of what might have been......

So, I learned that you have to focus on more than just sex. Aren't ya'll proud of me for being so perceptive? Now, this leads to an obvious question - would I do the same thing again if I could relive this situation? I've thought about it a lot, pondered it, and even sought the Brotherhood's advice on this issue. The answer for me is.....

SURE I WOULD! In a second! Damn, how are we to learn important lessons like the above if we don't sin and see the error of our ways? At least if you sin and learn from it you do better down the road. And how boring would life be without a little sin? It would be like watching a soap opera with only good people in it - what a dull crock of crap that would be. So, my motto is, "Sin and learn." Given some of my past transgressions, I think I am fast becoming an Einstein......

CHAPTER 2

STINK PERFUME

One of the biggest technological advances of the 20th century was the creation of stink perfume. I'm sure there are a few of you out there that may be unaware of this wondrous product. Simply put, stink perfume has been a staple item of novelty item and trick shops for years. Typically, it is sold in a one or two ounce bottle that has a pretty cheap looking phony perfume label on the outside. The liquid inside has a yellowy look to it. All this ambiance leads you to the big kill, which is what happens to your nose when you whiff the contents. It stinks like hell! This stuff has an odor than just reeks of a super rotten sulfur type smell. It will almost make your eyes tear up! Another thing that is good about this stuff is that you can open the bottle and it will only take a few minutes for its pungent aroma to fill the room.

My first brush with stink perfume came when I was in the sixth grade. My mother was going on a shopping trip to Macon and asked me if there was anything I wanted. I told her to pick me up something from a trick shop (if she happened to pass by one). I really didn't care what she got me as long as it came from a trick shop.

My mother went to Macon that morning and returned around mid-afternoon. When she got out of the car, I almost pounced on her in my haste to know what she had bought for me. She reached into her pocketbook and pulled out a small bottle.

I looked at this bottle and felt that I had really been shortchanged.

I mean, what could be so great about this tiny little bottle of yellow stuff? My mom, seeing the profound look of disappointment on my face, told me to open the bottle and take a deep whiff of what was inside. I did this and nearly broke into tears from the intensity of the stench! This stuff smelled like the guys at Homer Chambliss' General Store did in the evening when they had been playing cards and drinking beer for awhile. It was putrid! I instantly realized that my mother had gifted me with something that had far greater potential than either gold or silver. I was really gonna embarrass somebody good with this stuff!

Before launching the use of the product on a wide-scale basis, I felt that a niche market test was the appropriate starting point for this wondrous essence. I took the bottle with me to school one morning. On this particular morning, for some reason, the school bus driver was sick or something and my dad had to take my brother Ernest and I to school. Ed Jr. loaded us up and then picked up a couple of the Justice girls, who lived down the road from us, and then went on to pick up my cousin Frankie. On the trip to Forsyth, we were all wedged in that car pretty tightly. It was winter too, so all the windows in the car were up. I was sitting on the far right of the passenger side in the front seat. I silently reached into my jacket pocket as we drove and eased out the bottle of stink perfume. With an almost imperceptible motion, I got the top off the bottle. With the heater running in the car five minutes didn't have to pass for it to be filled with a vile and putrid odor.

I couldn't help but glance around trying to detect the level of nasal discomfort in the car. The Justice girls, in the back seat, were pretty straight-faced but you could see them occasionally scrunching up their noses. My brother looked like he wanted to bust from either the urge to laugh or to exhale! Frankie was softly laughing in the front seat and I was looking out the window trying as best I could to look innocent.

A few more miles went by and Ed Jr. cracked open the window, claiming that we must be catching the downwind breeze from a paper mill. When he said this, Frankie and Brother and I burst out laughing. The Justice girls continued to be somewhat quiet and appeared to be puzzled over just what was going on. I know they smelled that perfume though - I kept seeing one of them crack their window open and take deep breaths.

When we got to school, my dad let the Justice girls out and asked Frankie, Brother, and I to hang around. Glaring at the three of us, he looked us all square in the eye and exclaimed, "I just want to know which one of you little shits farted in that car?" We all swiftly protested our innocence and reminded him that it was not impossible that the Justice girls could've been the guilty parties. My dad said that this was highly unlikely and then we broke in and told him that we were gonna be late for school. That broke up this delicate discussion.

In my first period class I was elated. This stink perfume was great! It smelled to high heaven and then some. With this first test of its powers a success, it was now time to try out this magical essence on an even larger audience. I thought about how to do this and quickly came up with a plan.

That same afternoon I got on the school bus home and made sure that I sat far to the rear of the bus. My reasoning for this was purely scientific - I wanted to see how far and fast the aroma would spread once I uncorked this magic potion.

I waited until we got underway and were moving. Then, I eased the bottle out and let the formula do its work.

The time of year, as I mentioned earlier, was winter. This meant that the windows of the bus were closed. Once again within five minutes that bus smelled like a sulfur factory! I laughed until tears came to my eyes. Comments were wafting around the bus like,

".....somebody died....."
".....who had beans for lunch?......"
".....somebody ought to claim that - I'd be proud of it!......."

My brother Ernest (I call him Brother), who has a somewhat weak stomach, began gagging and sticking his head out the bus window (this was similar to an incident we experienced in the first grade. We - Frankie, Brother, and I - were sitting on the bus one day and Frankie cut the cheese. It was the worst fart I have ever smelled in my life - to this day I can remember my eyes burning, my nose feeling totally violated, and the seniors on the bus threatening us with physical harm.

My brother not only gagged, but opened the window in 20 degree weather and stuck his head out. Even though this act brought threats from some of the big kids on the bus, Brother said he didn't care. He said it would be better to die than to have to breathe that fart.)

Anyway, back to the school bus and the stink perfume, the remarks were beginning to fly about who was responsible for the rotten egg odor. Many potential culprits were accused and called out on the bus. It got so bad that the bus driver, my uncle Jerry, stopped the bus and pulled over. He walked back to me and asked me for the bottle. In one of the most heartfelt acts of my life, I turned it over to him.

The dejection I had felt over losing the bottle vanished when Jerry gave it back to me when I got off the bus one day a week or so later. I took the bottle in the house and showed it to my dad. I explained to him that this was the stuff we had unleashed the day we had the Justice girls and Frankie in the car with us. Ed Jr. smiled and asked if he could borrow the bottle? I said sure - proud that I had something that my father would actually like to use! He walked away with it and I could not help but wonder what he was gonna do with it.

I found out the answer to that question in a couple of days. Remember when I said earlier that one of the things the men in Juliette did at nights was to go hang out at Homer Chambliss' General Store? My dad took the bottle of stink perfume with him one night to one of these gatherings. Even today when he tells this story, it still brings smiles and some laughs with it. Ed Jr. walked into Homer's store and saw several of the guys standing around watching a game of poker. They were intensely watching the hand being played. My dad eased out the bottle of stink perfume and put a couple of drops on Alfred Smith. Now Alfred at this time in his life was about twenty-two or twenty-three and might've carried one hundred fifteen pounds on his six foot frame. In more precise terms, Alfred looked like a walking stick. One known fact about him was that he could eat anything he wanted and never gain any weight. My dad reasoned that this fact alone would make him the perfect target for his stink perfume assault. Ed Jr. dribbled a few drops of the stuff on Alfred's jacket, left the store, and walked out to his car to put the bottle in the glove compartment. After doing this, my dad returned to the store. (He estimated that he only spent about one to two minutes putting away the perfume before he returned to the store).

Ed Jr. said that before he even got back inside Homer's store that Alfred was taking verbal abuse. The remarks went along these lines:

"....Alfred, you stinkin' bastard...."
"....I told you about eatin all those damn pork rinds...."
"....I didn't work hard all day to smell your rank farts...."
"....damn, Alfred I can't even drink my beer!...."
"....somebody open a window...."

Alfred, as my dad reported, was red in the face and very vigorously protesting his innocence. This did him no good as every time he passed by someone they got a good whiff of the perfume. In fact, Alfred was asked to leave in a few more minutes. As Homer Chambliss said, "A man can't help fartin', but I can help where he farts! And the one place he won't fart is in my store on a Tuesday night. Alfred, get your stinkin' ass out of here!" With these tender words tossed at him, Alfred left and decided to call it an evening.

The next day Ed Jr. gave me the stink perfume back and agreed that it was great stuff. I forgot about it over time, and the stink perfume episode slowly passed into the shrouds of history......

That is, until 1972. For some reason in 1972 (I was sixteen), I was in Macon one evening and went out to the Westgate Mall. Come to think of it, I think I was out on a date with Jenny. Anyway, we were walking through the mall when I saw a small novelty shop. I wandered in and glanced around. On a small rack sitting on top of the counter where you paid for your stuff there sat several bottles of stink perfume. Unable to resist temptation, I quickly purchased a bottle. It was small enough to put in my pocket without arousing Jenny's suspicions (I forgot to tell you - while I was doing this Jenny was in a little shop across from this one. I think it was a dress or cloth shop or something). Anyway, I pocketed the goods and Jenny and I went home.

The next day I cued my brother in on the find that I had made the night before. We talked very seriously for several minutes about how to use the stuff to its best potential. After some discussion, our plan was in place.

It was a tradition at our house every Sunday for Ed Jr., Brother, and I to watch NFL football together. In fact, it was almost a religious experience for the three of us. We would gather every Sunday, load up with snacks and drinks, and proceed to watch the Falcons get demolished by whomever they happened to be playing on that particular week. Even though we knew that our butts were going to get handed to us, it was still fun to watch. What made it so much fun was the reaction Ed Jr. had to the games. My father is probably one of the most competitive people I have ever met. If he plays ping pong he plays to win. In fact, he would tell me, "You can talk sportsmanship all day long, but show me a man who accepts losing and I'll show you a damn poor excuse for a man! In fact, someone that doesn't take losing hard must be a Democrat because they are used to it!"

Anyway the Sunday that my plan went into effect the three of us were sitting there watching yet another Falcon annihilation. Around the start of the second quarter Ed Jr. rose from his chair to go get a glass of tea from the kitchen. While he was in there, I eased out the stink perfume, took the top off the bottle, and sat it under my dad's chair. Ed Jr. came back in the den, sat down, and continued watching the game. It didn't take long for the sweet essence to fill the room. I glanced over at Ed Jr., trying to keep from laughing out loud, and couldn't help but notice the puzzled look he had on his face. After a few minutes, he looked over at my brother and I and asked, "Did somebody slip one?" We both laughed but assured him that we were not guilty. A few more minutes went by. By then, the den was smelling somewhat like a sulfur production facility. My dad got this real look of disgust on his face and said, "I'll bet I've got to dig that damn septic tank up again!" At that, Brother and I burst into laughter. Ed Jr. then emphatically stated, "It may be funny to you shits, but it's a real laugh digging up that septic tank!" At this, he went outside and got his shovel. Brother and I 'fessed up to our mischief just as he was about to shovel the first spade of dirt out of the ground. Needless to say, Ed Jr. didn't appreciate our joke but the relief he felt over not having to dig up the septic tank far outweighed any bad feelings he felt toward my brother and me.

What important items can we say we've learned from this chapter? One, stink perfume can really spice up one's day-to-day living. Two, be prepared for fierce expressions of disgust whenever you utilize stink perfume. Three, seriously question anyone who cannot grasp the humor potential of this magic elixir. They obviously have a severe psychological problem. Try it and you'll be telling better stories than this at the next party you attend, make no mistake about it.

Now, I've done it. I've written a chapter on stink perfume. Shame on you Hughie, for not believing that I would write about it.

CHAPTER 3

CATCHING THE CHOIR LEADER
WITH HIS PANTS DOWN

I had my first brush with small town scandal when I was about thirteen years old. It seems that there was a rumour going around Juliette involving two prominent members of the church. Apparently, as the local buzz had it, the choir leader was holding extremely close and personal choral sessions with a lady in the choir - in fact this particular lady was featured in solos each Sunday and was easily the most prominent female member of the choir. I found out about all this while playing basketball in the back yard with Ed Jr. and Brother one day.

"You know, I get pretty damn tired of seeing ole' Ralph up there in front of the church each week talking about his relationship with God! I mean, he has some right..." spat Ed Jr. "Why shouldn't the choir leader talk about his relationship with God?" I naively asked him. "Because he's drilling 'ole Doris in the choir, that's why! He's doin' that and then wants to talk to us about his relationship with God! What a joke!" replied Ed Jr.

I got the distinct impression at this point that my dad was not referring to drilling for oil - he meant that Ralph was sinking the Titanic with Doris, queen bee of the choir! I couldn't believe it! "Dad, are you sure?" I asked. "Son, I'm pretty sure it's true, but I couldn't swear to it." replied Ed Jr.

A few weeks later my dad came into the house late one evening and exclaimed to my mom, brother, and I, "I can swear to it now!" I really didn't know what he was talking about but the story did unfold over the next several minutes. Apparently Ed Jr. had been in the cow pasture that adjoined our house (I meant it when I told you that I lived in the sticks) because he was working on a section of fence that was torn down. He had worked on it until it was almost dark. Around eight-thirty, he saw some car lights in the distance. He slowly eased his way through the pasture until he got to a clearing where he could make out just exactly what the lights were. "And I'll tell you, there was that damn Ralph's car and Doris was right in there with him!" Dad exclaimed. At this point my mom stepped in and said, "Edward, I'm sure the boys don't need to hear this!" My dad agreed and banished both of us to our bedroom.

Now there was no way in hell that my brother and I were going to miss this story! We slipped down the hall so that we would be close enough to hear. We really didn't need to do this though - Ed Jr. was in full voice and was making his feelings loudly known.

"Barbra, I was close enough to hear them! They both got buck naked and got in the back seat. After that, asses and elbows were flying!" My mom said, "What are we gonna do? If this gets out, it'll ruin the church." My dad was quiet for a second and said, "I think I have a plan." My mom inquired as to just what the plan was? Ed Jr. was mum for a second, but then said (rather quietly), "Let me just say that I think we can put a stop to this." My mom said that she didn't want to know what the plan was - given the schemes that my dad utilized over the years, this was absolutely the correct approach to take.

The next Wednesday evening Ed Jr. appeared to be quite animated even though he had had a hard day at work. Around eight-fifteen he motioned for me to follow him into the garage. I walked in there with him and asked what was up? He said, "Boy, have you ever heard of shining deer? I replied, "No Dad, I can't say that I have. What is it?" "Boy, sometimes some of these ole' boys will go out at night in their trucks and have their rifles on the seat next to them. They'll drive along real slow on the back roads with their headlights off. Every now and then they'll turn on their lights. If a deer is around, it'll get blinded by those lights. When that happens- BLAM! One shot and you've got a deer!" Naturally I asked my dad if we were goin' shining for deer. "Something like that son." he replied.

We got in our car and went down the dirt road towards Juliette. Then at the end of that road, we turned right and drove towards Marvin Bowdoins' store. When we got to that intersection, we turned right again and rode a few hundred feet up Highway 87. Ed Jr. cut on the blinkers to turn right when it dawned on me that we were going down the hill into the bottom where Doris and Ralph humped each Wednesday evening! And it hit me that it was also Wednesday night! I asked my dad if they would be at the bottom of the hill. "There's only one way we'll know the answer to that son." replied Ed Jr.

My dad cut the lights off on the car and we eased along at barely five miles per hour. You could faintly hear the gravel crunching underneath the tires as we crept along. The suspense was tremendous - I was dying to see whether or not Doris and Ralph would be in the bottom bouncing heinies! It seemed like it would take us forever to get there.

We crept along, inch by inch, until I could faintly make out something metallic at the bottom of the hill. As we inched closer, this metallic blur took form and revealed itself to be a car - Ralph's car! I strained my eyes trying to see what was going on inside that car. As we got closer, my eyes widened! I could see Ralph's ass peek up over the top of the seat, then go down. Up again, and down. Doris meanwhile was calling out to God and crying and stuff. Ed Jr. looked over at me and whispered, "Isn't this a hell of a note?" I was amazed at two things in this situation - one, I was seeing live sex in person. For a thirteen-year old country boy, this was a HUGE deal. Two, I found it totally incredible that people in their forties had sex. At that point in life I figured that all people did was rub liniment on themselves and drink coffee and stuff. These people were really gettin' down!

My dad surveyed this tender scene for about thirty more seconds. "Damn, enough is enough!" With this exclamation, Ed Jr. turned on his bright lights and laid down on the horn!

Since Ralph's car was only about twenty feet away from us at this point, I could see a scramble in the back seat that would've made Hulk Hogan proud! All I could see were asses and elbows! Ralph scrambled his withered old ass over the back seat into the front of the car and cranked it up. Doris threw a towel out the window - I don't even want to think about what that towel was used for. Ralph gunned the engine and took off. Dirt flew everywhere as the tires bit into the ground for traction. Ed Jr. then hit the gas himself and stayed right behind them. They drove faster and faster and then flew around the curb into downtown Juliette. I thought that this was the greatest thing - sex, a car chase, a cussing father - I was as close to heaven as I could get!

Ed Jr. ended the chase in Juliette because he was afraid that someone might get hurt. Plus, "I've made my damn point. Let's see what they do in church this Sunday!" he exclaimed as we turned the car around and headed back to the house.

It seemed like it took forever to go from Wednesday to Sunday. Of course, in a small town like Juliette an event like this doesn't stay secret for too long. Very soon afterwards the word spread far and wide about the goings-on at the bottom of the hill. Funny thing is, the spouses of Ralph and Doris seemed to have no idea as to what had transpired literally under their noses. The anticipation that built towards seeing how Ralph and Doris would behave in church that Sunday transfixed the community more than any World Series or Super Bowl ever could.

Sunday finally rolled around and my dad and mom were up early. Even my brother and I, who normally rose on Sunday morning like a pair of Frankenstein monsters, sprung out of bed and got ready for church. In fact, if I remember right, we were ready almost an hour before the services even started!

We all pulled into the driveway of the church and Ed Jr. was musing loudly about how Doris and Ralph would have to quit the church, or, at the very least, give up their lofty positions in the choir due to the events of the past Wednesday evening. Based on the number of cars that we saw in the parking lot our feelings that many people were aware of Wednesday night's activities were true. You know how when you attend church on an Easter Sunday that some people will show up who don't come again for another year? That's how it was this particular Sunday. I saw people I hadn't seen in ages - in fact some that I don't think had ever set foot in the church until this one Sunday.

Scandal sure seems to bring the people out. If ministers in churches with attendance problems were really smart, they'd stage a scandal every few months or so just to get the crowd built up.

We all hustled into the church to get a good seat. Even though we were early the church was already packed with people. It took us just a couple of minutes to get situated in our pews and we eagerly awaited the beginning of services. Actually, many of us were craning our necks trying to see if Doris and Ralph were in the church. Ed Jr. felt they wouldn't be in church at all. "No way in hell after what we saw, boy!" he whispered to me soon after we sat down.

About a minute or so before the start of services Doris bustled in — she was wearing a jacket and barely spoke to anybody there. She walked up to her pew and quietly sat down. Ralph came in about this time as well - he spoke to several of the men, including my dad. Ed Jr. was polite ("it is the church son") but was nothing more. Ralph went up to his normal pew and took his seat.

My dad was already upset and lo and behold, Ralph got up to lead the singing. As soon as Ralph stood up Doris scrambled up into the choir right behind him. In fact, Ralph started by giving a little speech to the congregation about judgment ("judge not, les' ye be also judged") and then broke into a solo rendition of "How Great Thou Art." Now, besides being guilty of singing a song that should only be sung by Elvis, Ralph also had the unmitigated gall to act "pious" yet again in front of the congregation. This four days after Ed Jr. and I had observed the two of them engaged in the back seat boogie! Doris, in the choir behind Ralph, was trilling away with the best of them. In fact, a couple of times she threw her head back and really belted the songs out (a similar position to the one I witnessed her in the previous Wednesday night, only the words she said then were different) with full religious fervor. It was a performance right out of Hollywood.

As we left, I had never seen my parents any more disgusted. In fact in a few weeks, amid great amounts of discussion, we left this church and went across town to another. We found contentment at our new church and I attended there until I was grown. To this day, my dad still goes to church there. Ed Jr. summed up this entire episode pretty well when we were reminiscing about it a couple of years ago. The conversation went something like this.....

"Remember when we smoked out ole' Ralph and Doris Dad?" I asked.

"Yeah boy."

"That was pretty funny, wasn't it?"

"Yeah, seeing old Ralph's white ass was pretty funny. But it was also pretty bad- them bein' such pillars in the church and all."

"Everyone falls short Dad."

"Son, I know that but I don't fall short and then tell everyone else how they ought to live. That's crap."

"I agree Dad but....."

"Look son, it's like this — that night gave you several things. One, it showed you that everyone falls short sometimes. It also shows you what being a hypocrite looks like. Ralph didn't live that down till' the day he died. And, last but not least, it led us to a church that we were happy and content with throughout the rest of your mother's life and one that I am still content with. The way I see it, ole' Ralph and Doris sort of did us a favor."

The way I see it, God does sometimes work in mysterious ways.

CHAPTER 4

THE VAPORS

Going back a little farther, I can remember being about eight or nine years old and playing outside in our yard. Ed Jr. had gone to my granddad's store to pick up some things and to stop by the post office. When he returned to the house he seemed particularly disgusted. I asked him what was wrong? "Al", he said (my dad always called me Al and I'll explain why somewhere else in this book, if I feel like it), "that damn Velma caught me at the Post Office and started telling me about all the ailments she has. All she's got is a damn good case of the vapors!"

Being young and thirsty for knowledge, I asked Ed Jr. just what exactly the vapors were? He explained to me that, for some reason, there is a certain segment of the elderly female population that seems to enjoy being sick and likes to elaborate on the tragedies surrounding the ailment (actually, Ed Jr. said it in terms a little bit blunter than this). Now before any of you women's libbers out there get upset and start taking this as a dig at women, let me affirm some points as regards my feelings towards the opposite sex:

Point 1: Women are infinitely superior to men. This is proven over and over again in IQ testing and other quantitative tests. Also, if you watch how we men fall all over women and humiliate ourselves in every possible way to impress them, then there should be no doubt as to who the stronger sex really is. I've told lots of friends of mine over the years that the main reason I married Debbie was because I was acting so damn crazy that I either needed to marry her or leave her alone entirely. Women are superior - period.

Point 2: Even if I didn't believe point 1, I wouldn't admit it. I live with two women.

Point 3: The following people were not women so we men can only blame ourselves: Adolf Hitler, Genghis Khan, Jim Bakker, David Koresh, Jim Jones, Lance Itoh, and any male relative or friend of Elvis' that wrote a book about him.

Point 4: (You can fill this one in yourself - I'll leave a blank area so that you can pencil something in. Once you do this, leave it lying around so that your wife will see it. If you don't think that you'll win points by agreeing with me here, you're crazy). The space follows

Okay, women are superior, but, no one is perfect, and the "vapors" are something that women will have to own up to. Anyway, back to the story. After hearing my dad's words, I started listening to some of the conversations at church, and at school, and at the store, and Ed Jr. seemed to have a point. There was Simulah Smith, who spoke of leg pains that a football player needing knee surgery would not experience. There was Aunt Booner, who made respiratory problem description an art form. Even today, there is a lady at our church that I refer to as "ole gloom and doom." I swear that this woman lives to be down and out with hers or someone else's problems. It doesn't have to be her problem(s) - she will gladly carry the cross for anyone who is suffering. If you see her coming after a disaster of epic proportions, like say a tornado or something, you'd better take off in the opposite direction as opposed to hangin around and being forced into talking with her. She could literally explain miseries for hours. Sometimes, you just wanna say, "You miserable little $%&#@@. Get a life!" But we don't dare say things like that for fear of offending the doomer/gloomer. Anyway, if someone would start a therapy group for moaners and groaners (vaporists being the scientific term) we would all be a lot better off. I am personally willing to make a big contribution to getting this therapy group off the ground and running.

The best come back I ever heard anyone give to someone with the vapors was from my dad, Ed Jr. Remember Velma, the lady I mentioned a little earlier? One time I went with my dad to the store and then to the post office. Sure enough, there was Velma. Velma would stay at the Post Office for hours, literally commandeering anyone around to expound on her sicknesses. It always amazed me that a woman with so many problems had the stamina to stand up and explain them for hours. Anyway, we were in the Post Office and my dad, being polite, says hello to Velma. Velma says, "Oh, hello Ed. I'll tell you I'm having a bad time. A real bad time!". "Sorry to hear that, Miss Velma", said Ed Jr. "Yes", Velma said, "I been up the past few nights with bad pains in my back, legs, buttocks, and neck. The liniment doesn't work, the salve doesn't, nothing works. It got so bad I went to see Dr. Bramblett yesterday. You know what Dr. Bramblett said?" Ed Jr., letting chivalry override common sense, said "What?" "Dr. Bramblett told me that I've got pus on my kidneys. He said that if this here medicine don't work, they'll have to drain it off in a surgery! Lord-a-mighty, what am I gonna do?"

My dad, who was about an hour away from eating lunch, literally looked like he could wring Velma's neck. He looked at Velma and said, "That's the filthiest damn thing I've ever heard! Why would you think that I would give a shit about puss on your kidneys? Or anybody else's? Either get healthy or stay at home if you're in that bad a shape!"

The vehemence of the words, and the sincerity of them, struck home. Velma left in a huff, and I scarcely remember ever hearing her complain about her miseries again - at least around Ed Jr. My dad later on told me that you have to handle people like Velma firmly or you'll spend the rest of your life listening to them moan and groan. And, as Ed Jr. succinctly put it, life is too damn short to bother with the vapors. Of course, the moral of all of this is - avoid, like hell, those with the vapors. If more people would use the Ed Jr. approach to this malady, the world would be a much nicer place to live in.

CHAPTER 5

THE BROTHERHOOD

You may note at this point in the book that I have told some less than flattering stories about myself. Now though, it is time to brag a little. It is time for self-glorification. It is time readers, to reveal to you the existence of the most elite social organization in the world. More elite than the Royal Family, Palm Springs society, or the Four Horsemen. More elite than membership in the Augusta National Golf Club, ownership of an executive box at the Georgia Dome, or front row seats at a toughman competition. The organization I refer to is that one known collectively as the Brotherhood.

The membership list of the Brotherhood is set at three. That's it. Three. The first two members were inducted in 1956, the third in 1976. There has been over the years a consistent string of "wanna-bes" who desire membership but these foolish desires are routinely laughed off. In fact, these membership attempts are a great source of amusement to the current members. There is a Spiritual Advisor to the Brotherhood but, this is an ad hoc, or at best an honorary position within the group. Plus, the Spiritual Advisor of the Brotherhood is old as hell and, in all likelihood, will reduce the membership back to its core group of three at any time in the near future. So, the membership is set at three. And three it will stay, until we all croak.

First, you have to understand the individual members and what brought us together. Secondly, you have to understand our values and beliefs. Third, you need to understand what sort of activities the membership indulges in, as this will give you an idea as to the character of the group. Fourth, you need to understand that the concepts about to be expressed here are so profound, so unlike anything you've ever heard, so different from any other group that you're familiar with on the face of this earth that, even after reading this, you may not understand what we're all about. And frankly it's not important to us that you understand. We don't care. The only person who could give you any insight into what we're about (besides ourselves) is our Spiritual Advisor, and he has been instructed to never give out the karmic underpinnings of this group. We are discussing a few bare essentials about us only to give all of ya'll a slight clue as to what we're all about. And that's all it is - a very slight clue. Something on paper so that scholars hundreds of years from now will study this, trying to determine just what made us click, what made us what we were, what made us—the Brotherhood. We wish them the best as they try to figure out the intricacies of this elite group.

The Brotherhood actually began in Forsyth, Georgia in 1956. I was the first born and hold the cherished title of most senior member of the Brotherhood. Following my birth, just two days later, was the birth of Ray Pippin. Ray and I were born together, bunked side-by-side in the nursery, and went through elementary, grammar, and high school together. After high school, we attended junior college and college together. We got married within one month of each other and our spouses (there is a chapter devoted to Kendra later on in this epistle) are extremely good friends. I don't know whether or not I believe in destiny, but, if there is a such thing, I think it was in Ray's and mine to be good friends for life.

I can remember vividly a ton of things that Ray (actually, I call him "the Pip" most of the time) and I have done together. I will recount a few of them here to give you an idea of the relationship and how it formed the nucleus of the Brotherhood.

One time, in our ninth grade geometry class, the Pip walked into class with the look of a self-assured man. As he sat down he gave me a knowing look and slowly extracted a whoopee cushion from the inside of his notebook. This alone was enough to get me laughing but it was just the start of the festivities that were to ensue.

Our class was taught by a man named James Love. He coached the boy's basketball team and was an assistant coach on the football team. He actually was a pretty cool guy and handled the scene we laid on him this particular day pretty well.

Geometry at best was about as exciting as watching an Alka-Seltzer commercial and, on this particular day, it was doubly so. It was April, spring was in full force, and we only had a month or so left of school. Coach Love was diagramming an isosceles triangle on the chalkboard. Ray cut his eyes around to me and slipped the whoopee cushion out of his notebook. I watched him as he quietly dropped his head down and began blowing the whoopee cushion up. He got it inflated pretty good and looked up at me and winked. He crooked one of his legs up and eased the whoopee cushion underneath. The leg he crooked up was his right one, which could not be seen from the angle Coach Love had from the front of the classroom.

The Pip held this position for a few minutes. It was all I could do to keep from bursting out laughing from just wondering what his sinister scheme was. Finally, after a couple of minutes went by, Ray started rubbing his stomach and had a very pained expression on his face. Coach Love kept lecturing but began to notice that Ray had a very solemn expression going. Ray raised his hand. You could've heard a pin drop! Coach Love looked at the Pip and asked, "What do you need, Ray?"

Ray replied, " Coach Love, I don't feel real good." At about this moment, the Pip let his leg fall on the inflated whoopee cushion. It let out a Bronx cheer that sounded somewhat like a tuba symphony. The class collapsed in laughter. I can literally remember tears coming out of my eyes. Ray, in a display of true character strength, resisted the temptation to laugh and kept a pretty stoic expression on his face. Coach Love (who by the way laughed too) said, "Go ahead now, get on to the bathroom!." Ray looked up and replied, "Don't need to go......I feel much better now." Coach Love, in fear that the Pip was going to further embarrass himself and the class, ordered him to go to the bathroom.

I undoubtedly at that moment thought Ray was the coolest person that had ever lived. Not only had he gotten away with having a whoopee cushion in class, he had blown it up, sat on it, and even got some free time to go to the bathroom! He didn't even get in trouble! I guess Coach Love intuitively understood that free expression is an important right to protect, and, let Ray freely enjoy his rights.

The next year, in the tenth grade, the Pip came to school the Monday following Easter Sunday. It's hard to imagine the Easter holiday being a source of humour, but at this particular time it was. Ray showed up for class with a paper bag. I asked him what was in it? He eased it open and showed me a bunch of colored tablets, roughly about the size of aspirin tablets. When I asked what they were, Ray replied, "You know those tablets that they put into vinegar to make the Easter egg dyes? My mom had to dye a bunch of eggs for the Easter egg hunt at church. I brought these along because I thought we might have some fun with them."

I couldn't imagine what kind of fun, but as we walked down the hall, an idea occurred. We happened to walk by a water fountain - I asked Ray for some of the tablets. He gave me a few and I stuck one in the fountain. I found that if you tapped one of them in there securely enough that you could turn on the faucet and a stream of brightly colored water would emerge. This immediately opened our eyes to some humourous possibilities. It didn't take long for a plan to formulate.

Ray and I grabbed a couple of yellow Easter egg dye tablets and walked over to the water fountain that was just outside of the boy's bathroom. We looked around and fortunately there was no one in the hall. We reached into our pockets and pulled out some tablets. Ray's eyes lit up and he said, "Let's put in the yellow ones!" We took one yellow tablet each and stuck them into the water fountain spigots. Once this task was completed we decided to wait around and see what would happen. It took a lot of energy to keep from convulsing in laughter over this, but, somehow we managed to contain ourselves.

It didn't take but a minute or two for someone to come out of the john. We saw that this guy that was in either the eighth or ninth grade - can't remember which - plus I can't tell you his name as we didn't really know him well. This was probably all for the best. Anyhow, whom ever this guy was, he strolls out of the bathroom and pauses to take a drink of water before going on to his next class. He bent over, turned on the water, and the brightest stream of yellow water imaginable emerged! This guy literally jumped away back from the fountain and yelled, "What the hell's wrong with that fountain?" Ray, with the straightest face you can imagine, said, "There's been some plumbing work going on in the restroom. I'd be careful cause they obviously have connected up some of the wrong pipes!" I thought I'd fall down laughing. The crazy thing was - this guy believed it! He thought I guess, that he had just taken a swig of urine from some faulty pipes in the water fountain! I'll bet to this day he still tells this story to his friends and acquaintances (then again, maybe he doesn't).

I could go on and on and tell some similar stories involving Ray and me (and I will) but I think it's important here to take note of a couple of things. First, there was and is a strong bond of loyalty between the two of us. Over the years we have both told each other things that could get either one of us into a lot of trouble. Also, we have never argued about anything - I don't think we've ever come even close to one. In fact, there have been times that Ray's wife Kendra, who's a real good friend of mine, will tease me about something (I love to get teased and Kendra will tell you that I give it back to her in spades) and Ray will sort of defend my honor. It's like we go to whatever extreme needed to protect the friendship. Ray is one of my two best friends and there is very little I would not do for him.

Secondly, another unwritten code between us is that we never dated anyone the other dated. This didn't just include people we went steady with or had strong feelings for but included one shot dates as well. It's like we never wanted to risk the friendship over feelings we had for someone we dated. In fact, one time Ray said that we could always find another woman to date but that we would not be able to find a similar friendship. This pretty well sums it up - I'll write a whole lot more about things we have done, but don't be mistaken about one thing. The Brotherhood represents the closest friendships that we have on the face of this earth. I've told many people, on more than one occasion, that as long as my immediate family and the Brotherhood are there that I can pretty much cope with everything else. This is especially true when you've worked in private business as long as I have. You very quickly find that most of the people you deal with are only your friends because of the company you represent, or what they think you can do for them, or whatever. I'm convinced that if everything went to hell and I had to pump gas for a living that the only people that would truly give a damn about me would be my immediate family and the Brotherhood. Because of that, they are the priorities in my life. And as of yet, neither has let me down.

Don't let this sensitive, serious stuff take away from the fact that the Brotherhood has done some pretty creative things in the pursuit of fun. Before going further with that, I feel it's now time to introduce the junior member of the Brotherhood, Hugh Foskey.

Hugh was born a couple of years after I was in Adrian, Georgia. One thing that you should quickly deduce from our backgrounds is we came from small, rural communities. I from Juliette, Ray from Forsyth, and Hugh from Adrian. The similarities in upbringings and values probably has more than a little to do with the success of our relationships. Also, the three of us have been relatively successful in business. Ray was the first person in the history of Georgia College (in Milledgeville, Georgia) to pass his CPA exam the first time he took it - at the tender age of twenty-three. At the age of twenty-eight he was a partner in the CPA firm of McNair, McLemore, and Middlebrooks. He and Kendra (and Nancy Kate and Ray III) live in a very exclusive neighborhood in Macon. Ray drives a Mercedes, and has a ton of investments going on in a variety of things. Hugh and Rosemary and their two sons (Ross and Will - Ross is named after famed wrestling announcer Jim Ross) live in a very nice home in Warner Robins. Hugh has worked at Robins Air Force Base for twelve or thirteen years. He has steadily risen through the ranks at the base and now holds the position of Section Chief. He has achieved all this at the ripe old age of thirty-six. I am currently the Human Resources Director for a large mining/minerals company. We employ approximately six hundred people at the site where I work. Debbie, Will, Alison, and I live in an older brick home in a nice old neighborhood in Macon. So in summary we all have done relatively well for ourselves, especially in light of our country kid upbringings.

The similarities among the three of us, therefore, are many. Our careers have taken a similar path. We all got married in 1981 within about six months of each other. We all have two kids. Most importantly - our values are similar. We would be shot dead before ever voting for a Democrat. We believe that the idea of taking money from people who produce and giving it to those that don't is abhorrent. We feel there is no better music than Elvis Presley, Buddy Holly, BTO, or the Guess Who (in fact, if either Burton Cummings or Randy Bachman ever happen to read this book, we would die to get your autographs. Your groups to us were like the Beatles were to other people). We love nachos with cheese. We make yearly treks to the dog track and love live boxing matches. Toughman contests are even better. We feel the best school in the world is Georgia Tech. This is true even though none of the three of us went there. We religiously go there to watch football and basketball contests several times a year. And even though we know University of Georgia fans and have some that are close to us, we would pull for Tech if Georgia beat them one thousand times in a row. Baseball is a also big thing for us (Braves #1), even though the idiots that run and play major league baseball have just about ruined it for us with the strike a few years ago. If I had a million dollar a year job, I cannot even imagine running home to tell Debbie that I was not working at it due to principle. Implying principles means crediting the person with the intelligence to have principles. And believe you me, for this reason alone, the players and owners can have no principles.

We believe that a Nu-Way hot dog was sent from heaven. We feel that any woman that ever cared about any of us should be put on a pedestal. We feel that the City Government in Macon, Georgia is the stupidest and poorest run in America. Last, but not least, we support and believe in each member of the Brotherhood. This is the SAFE refuge - one where you will not be let down, lied to, dissappointed, or anything else that's negative. I remember one time a few months ago a very close friend of mine invited me to join the Rotary Club. The Rotary in Macon is probably the most exclusive business club there is, just as it is in any other community. I turned the invitation down. When asked why, I merely stated that I was in the most elite social group in the world. When asked about that, I shrugged off the question and avoided giving an answer - the Brotherhood conceptually is a hard thing to explain. I'm having trouble here although I'm gonna trying my best. Remember this though - this is the only time any of the three of us will ever put anything down about ourselves in writing

- EVER!. So study and do with it what you will, cause this is it.

Back to Hugh - Ray and I first met Hugh in September of 1976. The first meeting was a little unusual. Ray and I had only been at the school a few weeks and really didn't know that many people. We went to the college's cafeteria for dinner one evening, ate, and decided afterwards to go into the rec room to goof around. We walked in there and noticed a pinball machine, a couple of vending machines, and other miscellaneous things. The thing that most caught our eyes were the two pool tables we saw over in the far corner of the room. We casually watched the people playing pool on the tables as they both were occupied. On one table we noticed this guy playing who looked a lot like Duane Allman. He had long, shoulder-length brown hair, and wore jeans and a tank-top. This was complemented with a mustache and a slow southern drawl. Ray and I struck up a conversation with this guy and his friend. It turned out that "Duane" was Hugh Foskey, the soon to be named third member of the most elite social group in the world. His friend was David Skinner, whom we renamed "Dirty" Skinner a short while afterwards. The "Dirty" nickname stood for the character "Dirty Harry" in the Clint Eastwood movies as we found that David loved those Eastwood movies.

As we talked to Hugh and Dirty, Hugh mentioned that he was having a bit of a hard time acclimating to his studies at Georgia College. He added, "I may only last a couple of quarters but that will give me enough time to pitch a couple of good drunks before I leave." This statement from Hugh was pivotal to his eventual entry into the Brotherhood as it told us a couple of things:

1. Hugh did not have an ego problem and, if he realized he wasn't doing well because he wasn't studying, it meant that he assigned full responsibility for his problem to himself, not to someone else. This is important because in the Brotherhood, dependency on anyone else to solve your problems is a no-no. You solve them yourself.

2. We knew that if he did screw up and get tossed out of school that those drunks we'd pitch would be fun. If the future is inevitable, and there is time to enjoy yourself now, why not? We knew that Hugh was a man with a mission.

Soon after this, we made one of our first forays out together as a group. Someone in my Economics class mentioned that the local Shakey's Pizza joint was having a dollar per pitcher of beer night. When I mentioned this to the Pip, he was all in favor of attending. And, almost as an afterthought, Ray said, "Let's invite Foskey and Skinner!"

We mentioned this to Hugh a couple of hours later in the afternoon, It took Ray and I about one second to convince Hugh and Dirty (who lived next door) to go to Shakey's with us. Thus planned, we went to Shakey's that night.

We went in about eight o'clock that evening and, as you would expect, the place was packed. Ray managed to sweet talk one of the waitresses into getting us a table. To do this for the Pip, this waitress had to rush a family out that was dawdling around after dinner (even at this point, the personal magnetism surrounding the three of us was kicking in). We got the table, sat down, and ordered a pitcher of beer.

All we ordered was one pitcher. You may wonder why we would only squander away one dollar after going through the effort to drive to Shakey's and to get this table. You have to remember, the three of us at that time were good ol' broke country boys. I considered it a good week if I had ten dollars in my pocket on Monday morning. We had to guard our money as best we could so one pitcher was it.

The waitress the Pip sweet-talked brought the pitcher out and we began to drink our beer. As we did, more people from Georgia College pulled up and sat down all around us. In fact, another table was pulled up next to ours so that we had probably twenty people seated at this long table. We were all casually talking when I noticed this one guy sitting a couple of seats down. He had a pitcher of Coke and the waitress, the one Ray sweet-talked earlier, was bringing him a large pizza! Our poor, hungry mouths gaped open as we observed this.

It turned out that this guy was Leon Killebrew. Leon (or Nub, as we nicknamed him later after observing him coming out of the shower one day) lived in Atlanta. He was adopted and apparently his parents had a ton of money. Leon had a brand new car and bought pretty much what he wanted to. Leon went on to become a close friend of mine, but, on our first meeting, he did not make a good initial impression. Anyway, Hugh looked at him, noticed the pizza, and whispered to me that if we struck up a conversation with this guy that it could lead to some free pizza. We talked for awhile and had to listen to Leon expound profusely on his likes, dislikes, and other items associated with his rich lifestyle in Atlanta. All of this gabbing was wearing extremely thin as my stomach growled and I got hungrier and hungrier. Finally, I looked at Leon (who had only eaten about two slices of the pizza) and said, "Hey man, how about a slice?" Leon never looked up and replied, "I'm not running a soup kitchen here!"

I got SO mad that I looked at Leon and said, "You're a stingy sonofabitch!" This silenced most of the conversation at the table. Leon looked genuinely hurt and stared down at his plate. Sensing the tension, Hugh tried to break it. He looked over at me and said, "Ed, say something nice to Leon." I looked at Leon, glanced at the others at the table, and said, "Leon, I hate your stinking guts. Don't bore me with any more of your bullshit!"

Leon got up, grabbed his jacket, and left. This was the break we were waiting for - he had left two-thirds of his pizza behind! Hugh and the Pip and I sailed into it. As we munched the slices Hugh looked over and asked me if I felt any guilt over what I'd said to Leon? I looked over at Hugh with a satisfied smile on my face and he said, "I guess not." Immediately after eating, we approached a small stage that Shakey's had over in the corner of the dining area. On the stage was a piano with a microphone on a mike stand. I got someone to play the piano as I coolly serenaded the crowd with an Elvis Presley number. Actually, from what I remember, we got a decent round of applause for our efforts. We went back to the table, shot the breeze some more, and then decided that it was time to get back to our dorms.

One problem I remember having upon leaving was that a lot of those people sitting at our table wanted to ride back with us (the early Brotherhood charisma rearing its ugly head again). We all got into this little Chevy Vega - we had three people each crammed in the front and back seats. This girl that was a friend of Hugh's, Jamie Jo, wanted to get in the car but there was no room. She said, "I'll sit in someone's lap, and I think it'll be yours Ed!" I, of course, was quite pleased with her choice and we took off for the campus.

As we drove up the road (it was now about midnight) we noticed a lone, solitary figure walking up the sidewalk. Upon driving closer to this figure, we saw that it was Leon. Apparently, Leon had ridden down to Shakey's with some friends but, because of his altercation with me, had decided to walk back to his dorm as none of his co-riders were ready to leave. Now the walk from Shakey's to the college was almost six miles (I don't know why I remember that but I do). We got close to Leon and Dirty, who was driving, and asked if we should stop and pick Leon up? Several said that we should and Dirty looked at me and said, "Okay Ed, what do you wanna do?" I thought for a second and said, "First off, there's no damn room in the car. Secondly, are we gonna offer a ride to a man that was starving us?" Dirty agreed, as did Hugh and Ray, and we went on home minus Nub.

One other notable thing happened on the way home. As we rode along I began to discover that I was really enjoying having Jamie Jo sitting in my lap. It was funny because I didn't know her at all but, there she was. She was talking a mile a minute about something to someone in the front seat. I leaned over and whispered to Hugh, "What kind of girl is she? The marrying kind or the puttin' out kind?" Hugh said, "She's a very nice, sweet girl." In my semi-drunken state, this was all I needed to hear. As she talked and talked, I slowly slid my hand up and firmly grabbed one of the cheeks of her butt. Surprisingly enough, she did not object to this, but smiled and said, "If you want to keep doing that, you're gonna at least have to invite me out to dinner and a movie." I removed my hand and we returned to the dorm. She got out, leaned over to me and said, "I expect to hear from you. " As she walked away, Hugh asked, "Are you gonna ask her out?" I stated, "I don't know." Hugh said, "Hell, you can't. One, do you really want to spend money on her? Two, is she someone you want to have a relationship with? And three, there's a talent contest at a local bar that will cost us five bucks to enter. We don't have the money for you to date Jamie Jo and enter the talent contest. I think you ought to enter the contest."

Hugh was right of course, as he typically is. When I asked him later why he felt this way about the issue, he was very to-the-point. "First", Hugh stated, "There's no way in hell that you could really give a damn about Jamie Jo. Second, the payoff on the talent contest is fifty bucks. Imagine what we could do with that! And third, is she someone you want to spend a lot of time with? Cause I know her, and if you get tied up with her, you're gonna be stuck for a long time!" "So, you're saying let her walk?" I asked. "Damn right" replied Hugh. "Anyway, if you win this talent contest there'll be more women than you can shake a stick at!" Shrewd observations - and Hugh brings this talent to the table time and time again. It's no wonder that he's recognized as the thoughtful, pensive member of the Brotherhood.

The talent contest episode did happen and it helps gives more insight into the developmental years of the Brotherhood. It so happened that one Monday night in the dorm some of the guys had come in from a road trip to Macon. They mentioned that one of the local nightspots, Bananas, ran a talent contest every Tuesday night. First prize was a trophy and fifty bucks! Believe you me, fifty bucks to us was like a king's ransom. The Pip immediately said that we would be entering. I asked, "What do you mean, we?" The Pip then stated that since I had been listening to Elvis records for years that it was only natural that I should sing in the talent contest! I told the Pip that I had never performed in front of an audience in my life. Ray said that that would only make it better - he promised that he would take care of everything and that all I had to do was sing the song. When I turned to my other brother Hugh, he merely gave me a pensive look that let me know that my fate was sealed.

Tuesday morning came quickly enough. My stomach was churning and I didn't sleep very well. Of course the Pip and Hugh had very restful nights. Just the thought of getting up in front of an audience and singing was hard for me to comprehend. What made it even worse was that Ray and Hugh liberally spread the word around the college about the contest. Because of that by the end of the day we had a group of thirty to thirty-five people who were going. At this point, I was so nervous and pissed that it would've taken some prescription strength sedatives to calm me down.

The evening too quickly came. First issue - what in the hell do you wear to something like this? Obviously, if singing an Elvis song was my "talent" then I needed to somewhat "look" like Elvis. Fortunately, I did have a decent crop of black hair and I was skinny (this was 1977 remember). I looked in my closet and saw one long sleeved white shirt that was made out of some sort of rough-to-the-touch type material. It had sort of the Elvisy look, but, I had no pants that really matched the shirt. As fate would have it Dirty Skinner walked in, looked at my shirt, and said, "I have a pair of white britches made out of the same cloth as that shirt!" Greaaat - now I have the outfit - Nub even loaned me a white belt which made it complete. I washed my hair and quaffed it up and put this stuff on. Even I had to admit that I did have a little of the Elvis "look" going for me.

It was getting around eight o'clock in the evening. The Pip announced that it was time to rock and roll (in this case it was meant literally). We all walked down the stairs towards the large lobby in the dorm.

You have to understand that this lobby was really big and a lot of people hung around in it because it connected both the girls and guys buildings. It didn't really hit me until we got closer to the lobby that this was a pretty weird scene. Here I was, all dolled up like Elvis, and with me was the Pip, Hugh, Dirty, and a couple of other guys. We were walking together looking like the Towaliga River Mafia or something. Anyway, I got some shouted comments from the crowd in the lobby, an off-color comment or two, and even a phone number from one girl. At this point, mild hatred towards Ray and Hugh would scarcely disclose how I was feeling inside. I was scared!

We all rode together to Macon and of course, the Brotherhood built the mood up with comments like, "That fifty dollars would sure be nice. Don't screw up!" ...or..."I'll bet a lot of real dorks have won the prize. You'll have a decent shot, E!" With encouragement like that, I should've been headlining Caesar's Palace, not worrying about a mere nightclub talent contest.

By the time we pulled up at the club, I would've eaten a fire ant sandwich to avoid having any part of this scheme. But, with all the people that had shown up from Georgia College, I knew that I was going to have to make my singing debut.

We all walked inside and got about six tables, which enabled all of us to sit together. After killing some brews and shooting the breeze, the DJ at the club announced that it was sign-up time for the talent contest. The Pip, true to his word, went up and signed me up for the competition. The moment of truth was not that far away.....

One thing that really helped me through the next twenty or so minutes (which seemed like ten years) was the fact that the many people from GC who came to watch this spectacle were quite supportive. Most seemed to sense the situation I was in, especially as I was quite open about sharing my plight with them. In fact, I even got a few kisses from some of the prettier girls there for luck, which made me start to realize why rock'n'roll was so popular among the local bands that played at these clubs. I kept trying to tell myself that this experience might not be so bad after all.

The Pip said that he had signed me up to be about the fourth or fifth act to participate in the contest. If I remember right, there were about twelve acts entered. Ray's reasoning for signing me up to sing fourth or fifth was that he didn't want me to go on first because the crowd would forget us after so many other acts. In fact, the Pip had even considered having one of the people who went with us sign up for the contest so that there would be one less competitor. "We'll get old Pinkston, who can't do shit, and get him up there!" Pip said. I told Ray that: 1) We didn't know if Pinkston had talent or not and 2) We sure didn't know that I did! The Pip said not to worry, that he knew what he was doing. I frankly felt that Ray should've signed me up close to last but he said that it would be a mistake. "E, around the ninth or tenth act, these people will be so drunk that they will not possibly know what you did. Trust me - you stick to the singing and let me worry about the business end of it!" That's the Pip - already showing signs of the knowledge that has taken him to where he is in the accounting field.

The announcer called up the first act in the competition. It was some old thin-haired, forty-plus year old guy that had a voice that cracked like ice. If I remember right, the crowd booed unmercifully. That really got me nervous - this was not a friendly crowd, it was more like a feed-them-to-the-wolves-type crowd. I thought at this point that there could only be one good thing about this situation - if I bombed, I would never have to get up in front of a crowd and sing again.

Ole Pops left the stage amidst tumultuous boos and act number two was called up. This was another forty-plus year old guy trying to sing "My Way." First off, the crowd at Bananas was not a "My Way" type of crowd. They were a country and old rock'n'roll type crowd.

Secondly, the first act did not set the second guy up for success. The crowd even began to throw things at this guy. Boy, I was getting even more and more confident as this evening unfolded!

The one thing that over the years has always brought me solace during times of trial was the close relationship that I enjoy with the other two members of the Brotherhood. At this point, as I was getting ready to go on-stage, I looked for Ray or Hugh to get a last minute pep talk. I really needed it to get up there on that stage and do what I had to do. The odd thing was, as I looked around the club there was no sign of either the Pip or Hugh.

The third act came on - a young guy who played the guitar. He was actually pretty good and got a nice round of applause. I was panic-stricken by this time - I was about to go on and as of yet no sign of the Pip or Hugh.

The house lights dropped and the recorded strains of "2001- A Space Odyssey" started playing. I was astonished - the Elvis theme music! As I later learned, this was one more thing that the Pip had set up for my big performance. I was getting ready to walk up on the stage when I noticed Hugh and the Pip slip in through a side entrance. With more than a little relief, I walked up to the stage.

I couldn't believe the reaction as I walked up. I guess the music, the outfit, and the deep Southern appreciation for anything Elvis triggered a very positive reaction. The crowd applauded and whistled, even though all I had done was walk up on the stage. When I got there, I noticed a couple of things. First, because of the spotlights, I could see absolutely nothing. It would be like singing into a closet. Second, the noise the band made would block out any crowd reaction. This gave me mixed feelings - the positive side was that it would be like singing alone because you could neither see nor hear the reaction. The negative side to all this was that I would have no idea until the song was over what the crowd's reaction actually was. They might love me, hate me, or whatever. The only way I was going to know how they liked the song as I sang it was if tomatoes started bouncing off my head whilst on-stage.

I got up on the stage and the band leader asked me what I wanted to sing. Being extremely nervous, I decided to do a fast song so that my case of nerves wouldn't show quite as much. I told the band leader that I wanted to sing "Blue Suede Shoes."

He then asked me what key I wanted to sing it in? I didn't have a clue - I asked,

"Have you heard Elvis' recording of this?" He said that he had. I then told him that I wanted him and the band to play it just like that. He said,

" Sure, no problem", and laughed.

As I walked up to the mike I decided that if I had to be up there I would do the absolute best I could. This included not only singing, but performing some of the gymnastics on stage that made Elvis so famous. I figured this way the audience was either going to love me or hate me - there would be no in-between reaction for sure!

I grabbed the mike and spat out, "Well, its a one for the money!" The drummer hit the drums real hard. "Two for the show!" Another hard hit on the drums. "Three to get a-ready, now go cat go!" At this point, the guitar and bass players kicked in. The music was great. I just sort of let myself go. I sang, sneered, wiggled my legs continually (although this was as much out of fear as it was from impersonating Elvis), and actually loosened up far more than I thought I would. The whole thing passed by in an absolute blur. When it was over, I looked out into the darkness. The place had exploded into applause - and was I ever shocked! Even the leader of the band congratulated me and invited me to sing with his band whenever I wanted to!

I walked back to our table amidst many hugs and slaps on the back. Upon arriving, I saw Ray and Hugh. We all hugged each other in the excitement and, after taking a few breaths, I remembered to ask them where they had been before I had gone on-stage? The Pip said, "Well, you may notice in your car when you go out there that there could be a funky odor in it." This sorry joker went on to tell me that he had picked up a waitress at the bar and had screwed her in the back seat of my car! I asked Ray, "How could you do that?" The Pip stated, "Look, I had a good time, but I did it for you. After I screwed her, I told her to talk you up with the people around the bar so that you'd win the contest!" Good old Pip - always there looking out for my best interests. Hugh's story was even better - there had been this one old gal that had gone around all our tables before I went on and talked with me and Ray and Hugh. When she talked to me, Ray eased over and said, "Don't do it - you need to keep your mind on the contest!" Which, due to the great deference I have for anything a member of the Brotherhood says, I did. It turns out though that when she went to Brother Foskey he willingly accommodated her lustful desires. The only problem was though that when he took her out to my car (if a car had feelings that night mine must've felt like a bordello) the Pip was already in it tattooing the waitress. I'm sure at this moment Hugh must've put on his most pensive look and decided that another locale had to be discovered and quickly. Lying his ass off, he tells this girl that he is a nature freak and would love to do it in the grass behind the club. This girl, who had to be drunker than a tadpole in a blender, bought this and accommodated him. Hugh, of course, being the gentleman that he is, even apologized to me for the grass stains on his jeans when he returned to the club. And of course both the Pip and Hugh reminded me that at the moment of truth, when I went out on the stage, that they were there in the club cheering me. In this they must have been telling the truth because, as I mentioned earlier, they had greeted me as soon as I had walked off the stage.

This is the essence of the Brotherhood - fun, yet a commitment to duty. The members come first - all others second - even if a girl with the morals of a drunken salamander gets into the picture.

By the way, I won that talent contest. Between the Georgia College crowd and the patrons at the bar that Brother Pippin won over, it wasn't even close. I won a fairly decent trophy and fifty dollars plus the right to participate in the month-end finals. Believe it or not, I actually won the month-end contest and was invited to participate in the year-end finals in which the winner got several thousand dollars worth of prizes and some free studio recording time. I think I finished about fourth in that one. One thing that really hurt me in the yearly one was that my act was an Elvis impersonation and I won the previous contests right before Elvis died. By the time I did the year-end one there were probably twenty thousand nightclub Elvis impersonators out there performing. One thing that I did learn during this experience is that it can be hazardous to your health when you do an Elvis routine. It seems that many women go sort of nuts over anything connected with Elvis - even a two-bit impersonator like me. After these contests, if I was in this club and they had a "lady's request dance" (where the women ask the guys to dance), I would always get some two-hundred pound Elvis fanatic that would want to slow dance. Nothing like having about one hundred eighty-seven pounds of cellulite mashed up against you to make a man realize what some of the true hazards of show business are!

Another truly outstanding effort that cemented the future direction of the Brotherhood was the support we gave Hugh when he found true love in 1977. A girl that he liked named Donna Plough or Sow or something from Adrian (Georgia, Hugh's home town) enrolled at Georgia College that fall. The Pip and I immediately respected her. She wore old jeans most of the time and blouses that barely had enough cloth to quality as a semi-reliable handkerchief. She seemed to care about Hugh and I guess that's all that mattered to both of us.

There was a rule at Georgia College at that time that was called the "open dorm" rule. Basically what this rule meant was that on each Wednesday night, from seven p.m. until eleven p.m., guys could have girls up in their rooms. Basically, to the Brotherhood, what this meant was that Hugh was going to have Donna up in his room on Wednesday nights.

One Wednesday night Dirty Skinner and I were walking down the hall. Dirty had an eight-track tape copy of Bachman-Turner Overdrive's hit album, "Not Fragile." Now, I love BTO. I still feel that Randy Bachman was one of the most talented musicians that ever lived. And, not coincidentally, my favorite rock groups are the Guess Who and Bachman-Turner Overdrive.

Dirty and I were going to his room so I could borrow his BTO tape and listen to it for awhile. We got close to the room and I thought I heard a low, muffled sound coming through the wall. Dirty and I stopped and listened. In a few seconds we heard a feminine cry of "oh, God" followed by a pensive groan that could only have come from one person! Dirty remarked, "Dammit, I forgot! Hugh's in there banging Donna tonight." I was disappointed. First off, I felt that Hugh would have had far more fun with the Brotherhood than with this girl (by the way, if you're wondering where the Pip was this evening, he had gone back to Forsyth to visit his steady girlfriend). Secondly, I was missing out on listening to some great music on account of Hugh's filthy hormonal impulses.

One thing that I always liked about Dirty was his outlook on life - he was genuinely a positive person. While I was getting sort of steamed over missing out on my tape, Dirty remarked, "Hey, man. Instead of the damn tape, let's just listen to Hugh for awhile!" This seemed to make sense so Dirty and I stood around for a few minutes and listened to the muffled groans and wails.

This type of activity gets dull pretty quickly. Dirty said that he had something with him that would spark these tender proceedings up. He slowly reached into his pocket to pull out four inch-long firecrackers. I asked, "What in the hell do you want to do with those?" Dirty replied, "We'll light 'em up and put 'em under Hugh's door! That ought to heat 'em both up!" I thought that this was a fine idea. To make it even better, we got a bunch of pennies, stacked them in rolls, and "pennied" Hugh into his room. For those of you that don't know what getting pennied into your room means, I'll try to explain. If you take a door and push real hard on the bottom or top of it you will make a crack or opening between the door and door jam. If within this crack you insert a roll of pennies, you'll create a situation whereby whomever is inside the room cannot possibly get themselves out of it. The doorknob will not even turn if you do the job properly. Dirty and I thought that the experience of dynamiting Hugh and Donna in that room would be further heightened if they were in a situation where they could not get out when the bomb exploded. Dirty and I quickly scavenged around and got a bunch of pennies together (it was really amazing how many fellow dorm residents were willing to contribute to this noble cause) and rolled scotch tape around them to secure them in crude rolls. Since the hallways in the dorm were small, it was easy to sit down and have your feet touch the door to someone's room. Dirty and I started pushing the bottom of Hugh's door with our legs so hard to that you could hear the wood in the door splintering. I worried out loud to Dirty that Hugh would hear us. But, as we got quieter, all we could hear was the sound of Hugh and Donna's grunts, shrieks, and moans. (We really couldn't be one-hundred percent sure if Hugh was having sex or administering a tattoo to Donna.) Anyway, Dirty and I proceeded to penny Hugh in with enough pennies that would ultimately require the campus building superintendent to get him and Donna out of their pit of passion.

Once Hugh was securely locked in, Dirty produced the firecrackers. We slipped them under the crack in Hugh's door in a nice neat little row. I pulled out a cigarette lighter that had been loaned to me for this specific purpose and lit them. Dirty and I ran over to my room and stood in the doorway so that we could hear the explosion and aftermath. A few seconds went by...you could hear the lit fuses hissing....then suddenly.......BLAMMMMMMMM! The sound reverberated loudly out into the hallway.

Doors flung open as guys in their rooms came out to see what was going on. It was all very exciting but the best part was listening to the words of love being expressed from within Hugh's dorm room..."AUGGGGGGHHH!!!" was the first sound that emanated from Donna's mouth. You could also hear clunks as both Hugh and Donna fell off the bed onto the floor. Hugh's first words of tenderness were, "G— Dammit! I'll kill those bastards...." After these words, Hugh bolted toward the door and grabbed the doorknob. You could hear the futility of that knob being turned back and forth - Hugh couldn't have gotten out of that room if there had been a billion dollars out there in the hallway waiting for him! Donna, during all of this of course, was crying and kept saying, "Why would they do this?" Even Hugh laughed a little when she said that. (Note - for the uninitiated, it's a Brotherhood by-law that all gags, if they are really good, should be enjoyed even if you are the recipient). Now by this point in the festivities, a sizable crowd had gathered outside of Hugh's room and, like Dirty and I, were enjoying the camaraderie. (There is one other item that I need to mention here at this point regarding this episode - right before we lit the firecrackers, Dirty and I were decent enough to post a sign on Hugh's door that read, "Caution - Couple Inside Screwing!" I wanted to throw this in less any of ya'll out there feel that Dirty or I were anything less than totally sensitive to Hugh's needs during this particular situation).

This odyssey ended when the campus maintenance people came up and let Hugh and Donna out of the room. When they emerged, a loud cheer went up from the twenty to thirty people that stood outside. Hugh came out with a big grin on his face - Donna looked like she was ready to kill most of us. Hugh took her back to her dorm and then came back and regaled all of us with the details of what happened in that room after the firecrackers exploded. A good time was had by all and Hugh had once more revealed a side of himself that indicated that his character, actions, and beliefs were beyond the scope of most people. A trait that catapulted him directly into membership in the Brotherhood. And the only other thing I can think of to tell you about this episode was that for some reason Donna was markedly cool to the rest of us afterwards. I guess some people don't have a sense of humour.

Another thing that set us apart from most of those that we associated with was the fact that we had a good time but also did quite well in college. I already told you how well Ray did and Hugh and I also maintained pretty high GPAs ourselves. In fact our floor, the third floor in Napier Dorm, had the highest overall grade point average of any dorm floor at the college. We guys raised so much hell together and had so much fun (we launched the first panty raid that had been held there in years) that we were dubbed, "The Third Floor Raiders." We even had titles and responsibilities assigned and posted for everyone. My title was "Der Fuehrer" cause I thought up one or two of the crazy things we did. Ray was the Financial Advisor, Hugh was the Head of Security, and Dirty and Mike Stanley (who were not above smoking the occasional "j") comprised our drug enforcement bureau.

Chemical warfare is not a new concept but it is one that we employed in the Brotherhood. I'm gonna tell you this one last college Brotherhood story and then we will go on to the adult years. It is important that you understand these things as to even have a clue as to the formative underpinnings of this elite group. You can't understand why something is the way it is if you don't understand where it came from. Thus stated, we can move forward.

It's was May of 1977. The Pip and I were about two weeks away from graduating from college. Unfortunately, it was a Thursday night (the big party night at Georgia College) and was raining hard outside. Worse yet, we were both extremely broke. The end of college partying that I'm sure goes on everywhere has taken its toll on our wallets. About eight o'clock or so that evening a bunch of us were standing in the hallway shooting the breeze. After several minutes of this, one guy stepped out into the hallway. It was Big Al - an almost legendary character at the school. You'd have to see Al to get the full appreciation but the description here hopefully will suffice. Al was about six feet tall and probably weighed around one hundred ninety pounds. He had stringy blonde hair that was a little shaggy. His face was pitted with enough acne to replicate a topical map of Brazil. His extremely narrow shoulders were complemented with an ass that was almost Baby Hughie size (no slam to Brother Hugh, who has the sleek body proportions of an Olympian). Topping off this exciting package was a voice that sounded somewhat like a cross between Elmer Fudd and Dolly Parton. It was this person that stepped out into our hallway. Little did we know at this point that Al was about to cross over from being a person into the realm of legend.

The commentary in the hallway evolved around how nice it would be to have a cold beer. A friend of ours named Dan mentioned that he had some gin and Coca Cola in his room. Big Al blurted out, "I've never had a mixed drink before!" We all were astonished and Dan volunteered that he would be more than glad to fix Big Al one. Dan also recruits me to help him fix the drink - of course, being the humanitarian I am I quickly agreed and recruited Brother Foskey to come help us with this project as well.

We walked into Dan's room and watched as Dan produced the gin and Coke. What we didn't know was that Dan was also going to introduce one more key ingredient for the drink. With a Cheshire cat grin, Dan pulled out a packet of unflavored Ex-Lax tablets. Holding them aloft, he exclaimed, "Now, we'll produce the ultimate Thursday night cocktail!" This was the formula for the drink that we proceeded to mix:

1. We used a tall glass.

2. We poured maybe a quarter inch of gin in the glass. No more than this, though. There was no way we were going to waste good liquor on Big Al. We put just enough in so that the drink smelled like liquor. Remember, this was Big Al's first drink. No need to waste a bunch of good alcohol on him.

3. We crushed to a fine powder four unflavored Ex-Lax tablets. With the adult dosage being two for maximum results, this volume of laxative is sure to relieve constipation not only in humans but also

in most large animal species.

When we completed mixing this special drink, the three of us swore a solemn vow not to laugh and we then brought the drink out into the hall and handed it over to Big Al.

It was obvious that Big Al knew nothing about drinking as he turned the glass up and chugged it like it was Gatorade. At this point, if there were any thoughts about whether or not we were going out for the evening, they were quickly resolved. As the Pip put it, "Why would we want to leave, go downtown and pay money for entertainment when we are about to have a Vegas-type floorshow right here?" Obviously, you can't dispute this sound logic. Another sterling example of why the Pip's in the Brotherhood and holds the cherished position of Business Manager of the group.

Big Al downed the glass and stood around in the hallway for several minutes, listening as we all ran our mouths. I was about to burst from wanting to laugh but somehow I managed to stifle the impulse. After a few more minutes, Big Al announced that he had to go study and disappeared into his room.

When Big Al shut his door, you would've thought that about one thousand tons of air had entered our hallway from the huge simultaneous expulsions of breath that occurred. The laughter was raucous and I'm amazed that Big Al didn't catch on to the fact that something funny was going on and that it might involve him. For whatever reason he didn't catch on, and the night went on.

At this point, it would've taken an earthquake or bomb blast to get anybody to leave the dorm. We stayed and stayed and talked and talked in that hallway. Finally, after studying for about an hour, Big Al emerged from his room into the hallway.

Al charitably looked like a man who had been run over by a truck. Dan asked, "What's wrong Al? You look like you've been run over by a truck!" Big Al responded, "I don't feel too good." Dan asked, "What's the problem?" Al stated, "My stomach don't feel so good. I need some Pepto-Bismol." Now none of us had any but Dan, being the good Samaritan that he was, had a suggestion....

"Al, I have some Tang instant breakfast drink. It's pretty mild - maybe drinking some of it would help your stomach!"

Big Al instantly accepted the offer and Dan motioned to me to go into his room with him. Dan said, "We've got him on the brink. One more shot of Ex-Lax ought to do it!" I said, "You mean you're going to give him some more?" Dan replied, "Ed, do you want to do this right or do you want to leave the job undone? Either you're committed to this project or not!"

With the gauntlet laid down, there was only one thing to do and that was to help Dan mix up the Tang. He pulled out the glass jar that was about half-filled with orange Tang mix. We yet again pulled out a big former peanut butter jar glass and loaded it with water and Tang. When this concoction was mixed, Dan proceeded to break out four more unflavored Ex-Lax tablets. We ground these up into a fine powder and loaded the stuff into the Tang. Once again swearing ourselves not to laugh, we walked out and handed Big Al the Tang (or maybe we should refer to it as "Tang Plus").

Al chugged this mixture like a desert straggler at a Coke stand. Saying that he had some more homework to finish he once again retired to his room.

At this point the crowd in the hallway is up to forty or so individuals. In fact, as word of these festivities spread we began attracting guys from some of the other dorms. As fate was to prove, we did not have long to wait before Big Al left the world of mortality and entered the realm of legend.

A couple of minutes go by. All of a sudden the door to Big Al's room burst open! "OUT OF MY WAY!!!", Al screamed as he ran, full speed, down the hall. You could feel the wind coming off him he was moving by so fast. He sidestepped into our combination bathroom/shower room. We could hear the door to the stall Big Al was using bang open and shut. Then the groans and sighs of pain began.

What occurred over the next minute and twenty-two seconds (we really did time him) could best be described as a tuba concerto. Big Al was expressing himself in a big way gastronomically. We were all absolutely beside ourselves with laughter in the hall - in fact, I remember seeing one guy who never expressed much emotion laughing to the point of tears. He laughed so hard that he literally dropped to his knees.

After the one minute and twenty-two seconds there was one thing that could be said - we were all drained. The guys in the hallway were drained emotionally and Al was also drained, albeit in another way. In fact, Al was in somewhat of a dilemma - in a stroke of master planning, Hugh and Dirty had conveniently managed to remove all of the toilet paper from the bathroom before Big Al entered. I'll never forget Big Al hollering, "I need some paper!" Hugh said, "What, the Macon Telegraph?" "You know what I mean, dammit!" cried Big Al. Because of this blatant use of profanity, Dirty stepped in and informed Big Al that the roll of toilet paper had a two dollar surcharge on it. Big Al cussed about being railroaded but Dirty stood true to his convictions. Big Al coughed up the two dollars (although Dirty later philosophized that having to step into the stall to hand the paper over and collect the two bucks was akin to voluntarily entering the skunk cage at the zoo). Once his anal symphony concluded, Big Al staggered out and actually tried to act nonchalant about the whole thing. This effort was equivalent to Captain Smith of the Titanic trying to act nonchalant after striking the iceberg. After a few pithy comments (which I cannot remember) Big Al went back to his room. For the rest of us, it must've been another couple of hours before we got the laughter out of our systems and went to bed.

The next morning the Brotherhood went to breakfast together and reflected on the hilarious events of the previous night. We all agreed that the Big Al mixed drink/Tang episode was a classic. We got to the cafeteria, grabbed some breakfast, and sat down. After a few minutes of eating we noticed a dark, somber looking figure approaching our table. As this person grew closer, we saw it to be Mark Von Fossen. Mark was a German guy - very nice, but we really didn't know a whole lot about him other than he was Big Al's roommate. (On that account alone we had expressed numerous sympathies for him). Anyway, as Mark approached the table we could tell that something was troubling him. Mark grabbed a chair, sat down, and started eating in total silence. It was Brother Foskey that spoke first....

"Mark", Hugh asked, "last night was a classic, wasn't it?"
"Classic isn't the word I have in mind", replied Mark.
"Oh, what word did you have in mind?" queried Hugh.

"Pissed off - let me tell you asses something! The night was over with for ya'll when ya'll went to bed!. Me - I was up all night!" stated Mark.

Hugh asked, "What was the problem?"

"If your roommate got up every twenty minutes to take a crap, wouldn't that bother you?" Mark replied.

"Not if the situation was as funny as last night", said Hugh, "You need to lighten up Mark. If I remember the situation right, you were laughing as hard or harder than any of us - don't be a hypocrite!"

Mark agreed that Hugh was right. Once again the thoughtful, pensive member of the Brotherhood makes his mark - contributing, as always, to the betterment of the group and to society in general.

You might think that this story ended here but it didn't. We pulled this prank close to the end of the quarter. The day after Big Al consumed all those "mixed" drinks he had a history final to take at one o'clock in the afternoon. The building he had to take the final in, Beeson Hall, is four stories tall. Apparently, Big Al headed over to class at about ten til' one. As he completed walking up the first floor steps and got about halfway up the second floor ones, mother nature sounded an urgent call. The only problem for Big Al was that the bathrooms in Beeson Hall were all on the first floor! Big Al scrambled for the first floor - eyewitness accounts say that he was hollering, "Get out of my damn way!" As he got to the first floor, he could contain himself no longer and dropped a big load of guano into his shorts. Needless to say, having your shorts full of guano presents numerous difficulties when it comes to taking finals.

Big Al gamely walked up the stairs to inform his professor that he would need to clean himself up before taking the exam. He asked if it would be possible to take the test at a later time? The professor abruptly told Al that the test was being offered at this time only and that if Big Al didn't take it now he would just have to accept an "F" for the course. Given that option, there was only one thing that could be done - Big Al sat down and took the final with a load of crap in his pants! One can only imagine the sweet, summertime smells that were emanating from Big Al's posterior during the exam. He did complete the test, made an "A" in the class, and probably irreparably killed any chance of a future social life at Georgia College. After all, who wants to be known as the date of the guy that shits in his pants? There was one positive though - Big Al had etched his name into those of the immortals who have attended the college. To this day these exploits are still occasionally discussed and pondered over at the school.

Nineteen seventy-eight was a pivotal year for the Brotherhood. This was the year that the Pip and I graduated from Georgia College. As you can imagine, there was much sadness emanating from Brother Foskey regarding this inevitable event. After all, this magic bond known as the Brotherhood was now being torn asunder. At our going away bash we made serious vows over drinks to stay in touch with each other. These proved to be the truest statements we ever made to each other. To this day, without exception, we have continued to stay in close touch with each other.

Ray, Hugh, and I got married within about five months of each other in 1981. Our wives - Kendra (Ray), Rosemary (Hugh), and Debbie (me) are very good friends. Of course, they share a link that only the three of them can - they were graced by God to be married to members of the Brotherhood. This is their destiny and they carry it off with matchless to style and grace. The three of them do offer constructive comments to each of us at times, but, let's face it - why would you want to put eraser marks on a Rembrandt? The three of us keep moving on, having fun, and enjoying life.

What type activities do we pursue now - what are the acquired social tastes of the mature Brotherhood? The next few paragraphs will explain them.....

One day in about 1982 or 1983, Deb and I had the Pip and Kendra over for dinner. We grilled out or something and actually finished eating pretty early in the evening. While sitting around and looking through the paper, the Pip noted that there was something at the Macon Coliseum that evening called a "Toughman Competition." We didn't really know what it was, except that boxing was involved. This was enough for Ray and I to make the trip over to see what it was all about.

We got to the Coliseum and saw that it was set up for boxing. In talking with some of the people there, we quickly learned what a Toughman Competition was - an athletic event designed to promote mindless violence, gore, and destruction. Apparently, the rules were such that all the "fighters" (and this is meant loosely, I assure you) could not have had any sort of previous boxing experience. Add to this a series of three-round fights (complete with judges) that keep going on as long as you keep winning and you have a recipe for a series of wanton assbeatings. The Pip's face lit up (mine did too) as we thought about the possibilities inherent in this type of competition. Then, as we began to take our seats, one person in the crowd mentioned that there would be sixteen matches put on that evening. We were in our element!

We each got a beer to drink and took our seats. The way they physically had this thing set up was that there were some bleachers sitting about twenty yards from the ring. All the "fighters" sat there. The announcer would draw two names from the hat. These two individuals would be then called into the ring whereupon they would duke it out in a three-round fight.

The ring announcer began the evening by calling out the first two contestants - a young black man in his early twenties (who looked like he had been chiseled out of granite) and a middle-aged white guy who had a stomach that looked like a spare Goodyear tire. The Pip and I immediately placed a bet - Ray bet the white guy wouldn't last forty-five seconds. I bet that he would. One thing that I have learned since is that you don't bet with the Pip on anything unless the bet hinges on pure, random luck. If your bet is based on facts or skills or whatever, Ray will clean your clock.

The bell for the first round rings - the two "fighters" circle each other. The black fighter throws a couple of jabs. About twenty seconds into it the black fighter reaches back and sinks a solid right hand about five inches deep into the cellulite-laden gut of his opponent. The guy went down faster than a cornfield under a tractor blade. I gave the Pip his dollar and we analyzed what we had just seen.

Ray stated, "That was great! Did you see how fast that slob went down? Why would some lard ass like that sign up for something like this?" I agreed and then asked the Pip, "You realize this is wanton, graphic violence with no socially redeeming qualities?" The Pip said sure, reaffirmed how much fun he was having, and asked me if I liked it as well. I told him that America was the land of choice and that this guy had chosen to receive his asswhipping. With these salient points discussed, we settled back in our chairs to watch the rest of the evening's activities.

As the evening went on some things began to stand out. First, we noticed that some of the fighters waiting in the bleachers were not behaving as boxers typically would - we noticed one guy eating a sandwich and yet another sipping on a cool Budweiser! Obviously, psyching yourself for a fight can be a different process for different fighters. Next, we almost went insane as they would play the theme from "Rocky" every damn time a fighter was introduced. To this day, I still cringe when I hear that song even though it is a damn good piece of music. Finally, I noticed how easily people could cram their mouths full of hot dogs, beer, pretzels, and the like while some poor slob was getting his brains beat out. It stills seems sort of odd but to each his own, I guess.

More humorous episodes occurred in subsequent fights. After the third fight was over one of the fighters in the next bout was introduced. He bounded up the steps, grabbed the top rope, and jumped over it and landed nicely in the ring. This brought a ringing ovation from the crowd! The ole' boy who was introduced next tried to do the same thing - I'll never forget what he did! He was about five feet six inches tall and probably weighed about one hundred and fifty pounds. He had long, stringy brown hair that dangled in his eyes. When they called his name to come down to the ring, Ray and I started laughing cause we had observed this guy earlier sucking down Budweisers at a furious clip. The "Rocky" theme blared out and this guy approaches the ring. He bounded up the steps, and decided he would try to duplicate the jump-over-the-top-rope-thing. As he hit the top step, he grabbed the ropes and jumped. The only thing was when he went into the air he hung his feet in the top rope - this caused him to trip, rotate 180 degrees, and smash his face directly into the canvas. It was a classic piledriver! I thought the crowd would never stop laughing. I can remember the handlers helping the poor guy up - he looked like he had already gone four or five rounds before the match even started. His match didn't last one minute into the first round before one solid left jab put him out of his misery.

One other important thing we noticed during the night was that if there was not a knockout in the first forty-five seconds the fight would inevitably go the full three rounds. After the first round, the combatants would lean on each other and grimace for two more rounds. They would be so tired that they could barely stand up by the end of the match. I can remember one fighter's upset girlfriend telling him after one of these type matches that she was ashamed of him. In response, the ole' boy told her that if she kept talking that way that he would be forced to whack her one. His girlfriend looked him right in the eye and told him, "The only thing that could embarrass you more than you've already been is when I kick your ass. And right now, I could! You need to shut up and go home!" With this, the happy couple trudged off into the night.

The Pip and I went home that evening delighted in this new sporting competition we had discovered. A little later on we told Brother Foskey of the evening's events. As we described them Hugh looked serious and then smiled. Hugh then stood up, cleared his throat, and with a pensive note in his voice stated, "I'm in for the next one, boys!" We took a solemn vow at this point that the next Toughman competition held would be witnessed by all three members of the Brotherhood.

The next Toughman Contest came about six months later. Ray, Hugh, and I piled in the Pip's car (Ray nearly always drives when the three of us go somewhere - one reason for this is that the Pip drives a Mercedes. If you were going somewhere and could go in a Mercedes, what would you do? It doesn't take the Brotherhood long to answer this question). We all headed over to the Macon Coliseum to watch the evening's festivities.

We got there, purchased ourselves a brew, and took our seats. Thanks to some careful planning on the part of our pensive member Brother Foskey, we procured seats on the second row at ringside. From this vantage point, we could not only watch the matches but we could also hear every grunt and groan that occurred during the evening.

Ever hear the mushy sound that occurs when someone sinks a hard right hand into a cellulite laden gut? That's the sweet sound we heard in the first match - a typical toughman encounter. A young guy, about eighteen or so, matched up with a thirty-five something year old guy whose training regimen must've included lots of potato chips and beer. If I remember right the fight lasted in its entirety about sixteen seconds. In fact, other than the drubbing, the funniest part of the whole fight occurred when one of the handlers said to Mister Cellulite (who had just lost the match and his dignity in front of ten thousand people), "You showed good footwork in that fight!" How could he tell - it lasted sixteen seconds! I doubt that you could say that Fred Astaire demonstrated good footwork after only sixteen seconds!

One thing I noticed during this match was that I recognized one of the handlers - his name was Don Sapp. Don worked for the Bibb County Fire Department and was really into body building. I met him when he came out to our plant one day to inspect the buildings. The fire department periodically does this so that if a fire ever broke out they would already be familiar with the buildings and would be more efficient in extinguishing any fires. I struck up a conversation with Don as we went through the plants - he was a real nice guy and very easy to talk to. When I recognized him at the Toughman, I walked up to the ring and hollered at him right after Mr. Cellulite was being dragged out (as a side note, as if enduring an asswhipping isn't bad enough, Mr. Cellulite's wife was upset because she had apparently already decided where she was going to spend Mr. Cellulite's winnings. If I had been this guy, I think I would've driven to Mexico and forgotten about everything). Don and I shot the breeze awhile, and then he said the magic words, "Where are you guys sitting?" I pointed over to where our seats were. Let me here very quickly point out that at a Toughman there are tables and chairs that surround the ring. This is where the judges, round sign girls, and others connected with the competition sit. Don invited the Brotherhood to sit in these sacred chairs. I went over to the Pip and Hugh and told them - they thought I was kidding! I quickly told them, "You can sit here on your ass if you want to but I'm sitting up there." I followed those words up by taking my new seat. Seeing is believing - Ray and Hugh hustled up and took their new seats as well.

We are now literally sitting only inches from the ring itself - so close that we can slap the mat and touch the ropes! The next two fighters came in (once again to that damn Rocky theme) and to say that they were both a little long in the tooth would not be doing these guys justice. One of them had the classic Baby Hughie shape with big tattoos on both arms. (For some reason I can remember one was a vulture with the words "Bertha Sue" inscribed underneath). The other guy had just enough hair to put him in the same league with a grapefruit - a definite candidate for a case of hair in a can. The first round bell rang and after a little shuffling around, Bertha Sue whopped Baldie with a hard right hand to the gut. Baldie staggered and dropped through the ropes right where the three of us were sitting - we literally had to push him back into the ring. As Brother Pippin put it, "He's heatin' up my beer!" For some reason, we thought that pushing this guy back into the ring was great fun and really made us feel like we were integrally involved in the action.

Right after this one of the Budweiser reps walked up and asked us what we were doing at ringside? I informed the guy that Don had invited us to sit there. The guy paused for a second and said, "Oh—— by the way, do you guys like beer?" Of course, to Hugh and the Pip this was like asking them if they liked to breathe. Almost in unison, they replied, "Hell yes!" This Budweiser guy gave them decals to put on their shirts that allowed them to go to the Budweiser truck and drink all the beer they wanted - free of charge. My brothers took full advantage of this once-in-a-lifetime opportunity. By the end of the evening, both of them were proclaiming that this was the best overall experience of their lives - even better than their weddings or the last time they went to a baseball game.

We were to repeat the Toughman experience many more times over the years, until the same guys were fighting over and over. When it got to this point, the competitions in Macon ended.

It was while playing golf with the Brotherhood that I first learned about the concept of "Texas rules". We were playing at a nice country club in Macon when Brother Pippin mentioned, just before teeing off, that real men play golf utilizing Texas rules. When Brother Foskey and I inquired as to what Texas rules were, the Pip kindly explained them to us. It seems that Texas rules require that when you tee off your drive must clear the ladies' tee box. If your drive doesn't make it past the ladies' tee box you have to unzip your fly and dangle your member until you putt out the hole. Hugh and I were a little incredulous that the Pip would be willing to invoke Texas rules on a country club golf course. Of course when we said this, Brother Pippin responded,

"This place can't be too nice. We're out here aren't we?" We both had to admit he had a point. By now, our manhood (literally) was being questioned and we all agreed that we would play using Texas rules the rest of the round.

We got by a couple of holes with no problem even though the pressure you were under each time you teed off was incredible. I was afraid that I was going to shank a drive and have to dangle my weenie for the rest of the hole. All sorts of thoughts ran through my mind - what do you do to hide yourself from the golfers on the adjoining fairways, what if you got tangled up in your zipper, what if a mosquito bit you there, what if...? Fortunately, fate decreed that it was not I that had to dangle the sausage but that Brother Pippin, originator of the plan, would have to.

When we got to hole number fifteen, the Pip led off and hit a frozen rope, straight as an arrow. The only problem was that the shot only got a few inches off the ground. As it turned out, the ball struck a sprinkler valve and richoted back about two inches behind the ladies' tee box.

Hugh and I convulsed in laughter. The Pip, on the other hand, was calm. In fact, he unzipped his pants and withdrew the pink crusader. Without a grin on his face, he stated, "The really big laugh would be if one of you "twigs" had to do this! Hell, I'll probably get compliments or even a date from it!" This outburst only caused Hugh and I to laugh even harder.

Serious golf was forgotten on this particular hole. Hugh and I both laughed so hard that we each shot tens on this par four hole. Every time we'd calm down a little we'd look over at Ray - he was walking at weird angles on the hole because of the necessity of having to hide his dingus from golfers on adjoining fairways. In fact, we almost had a scare when someone Ray knew hollered at him from the next hole. The guy actually started approaching us but the Pip hollered that he had the flu pretty bad and for the guy not to come closer. This actually worked, which gives you an idea of Ray's pal's IQ, because if he was that contagious why would Hugh and I be playing with him? Go figure.....

Getting back to the story, it seems to me like we quit Texas rules after a few holes because the novelty wore off. There also was a rather cold wind blowing and even the Brotherhood has limits as to what it will do in the name of fun. (Especially when freezing our genitals is part of the " fun").

We go to the dog track at least once a year and give the state of Florida our hard-earned money. We also have the yearly Brotherhood Christmas get-together at my house (last year Brother Foskey came in, ate a little food, told me he was sick, and went outside and puked in my backyard. I forgave him for it - this is one of the benefits of being in the Brotherhood - we are very tolerant of each others foibles). Last year we got to watch an Atlanta Falcons game from a luxury box in the Georgia Dome. We couldn't help but laugh - three old Georgia country boys watching pro football from a luxury suite. Our hosts at this event were constantly giving us drinks and food and asking us our opinions on just about everything. Don't get the wrong idea though that we are smug or put on airs because of stuff like this. We actually are all still amazed that we get to do some of the things that we do. And we also realize that it could all go away, in the blink of an eye. But there is one thing that we know - as long as we have each other, we'll get through most everything there is and have a lot of fun doing so.

Now you have a little insight into the most elite social organization in the world. I know we're an impressive group and that there's much more that ya'll would like to know about us. But this is what you'll get for now. Maybe somewhere down the road it's possible I'll write more. Maybe....

CHAPTER 6

KISSING

Kissing is an important subject to write about. Kissing causes marriages, divorces, kids, happiness, heartaches, and a lot of other varied things. Memories of kisses can cause profound happiness or great despair for people. All sorts of things can happen in a person's life after they kiss someone. Before going further, let's be sure we all have a clear understanding of what the word "kiss" means.

For this literary work, kiss does NOT refer to the pecks on your cheeks and lips that you have received from your mom, your grandma, your teacher, or whomever at various points in your life. Kiss, for our purposes, refers to the real deal - tongue stabbing, spit swapping, germ moving acts of dental gymnastics that we have all experienced and enjoyed - what we really think of when we think of the word kiss! Pro class tonsil hockey!

At this point, you're probably repulsed by the kiss description I just gave. I know it sounds pretty gross but it is the truth - kisses basically turn two people's mouths into roller coasters with disconnected tracks. Thelips are gonna roll anywhere and everywhere all over the recipient's face - over the gums, teeth, lips, etc. Let's for the moment accept the premise that some things we like to think of as beautiful are profoundly disgusting. Don't think so?- walk up accidentally on a couple that are really kissing and note the feelings of disgust you experience ("can't they save it for the Motel 6", or, "look at him/her- I'd rather kiss a cow right on the butt!"). It's inevitable that we feel this way because we like to deny our baser sides unless we want to indulge them. Then its okay for us and our partners to turns our mouths into saliva guided helicopters- it just isn't okay for those other poor slobs to do so.

Before noting the great (and not so great) kissers of my life, I must acknowledge the ultimate kisser - my wife, Debbie. She still has what it takes to curl my toes up in this department (which is one reason we've been married for fifteen years). I really mean this, plus, I am about to talk about all these other women I have kissed over the years so I would be a damn fool to not put in a plug for the wife first. Just remember Deb that when you read this stuff, I married you. The others were nice but you are the one that I'll swap spit with throughout eternity.

The first real, honest-to-God kiss I ever experienced occurred when I was fifteen years old. It came from the first love of my life, a girl named Phillippa Stanton. Phillippa, at that time, was fourteen years old. I met her when she called me at my home on a Saturday afternoon to invite me to a party that she was giving. In fact, I can remember my mother answering the phone and coming back to my room saying, "Edward, it's for you. IT'S A GIRL!" (Like a girl calling me must be a mistake or she's headed to the insane asylum or something). I talked to Phillippa and made up some kind of lame excuse as to why I couldn't go to the party. The real reasons I didn't go:

1. I was terrified (no experience with girls).
2. I knew nothing about her and a guy's reputation had to be maintained. What if she was really like, Elephant Man ugly? Best to take no chances.

After getting off the phone and grabbing my high school annual, I realized what a stupid mistake I had made! Phillippa was beautiful - I could've kicked myself (I also was to find out later in the relationship that she was as beautiful on the inside as she was on the outside). I resolved to see her at school Monday and tell her how sorry I was to have missed the party and to please invite me to any future ones that she might have.

I did see Phillippa at school that Monday and my heart melted - if anything she was prettier and nicer in person than her picture in the annual suggested. If there was ever a case of someone falling for someone very quickly it would describe me as regards Phillippa.

I went over to her house a few times after that and it was obvious that we cared a lot about each other. Finally, one afternoon as we were talking I leaned over and kissed her. At that moment a gazillion fireworks exploded in my head! I think we actually kissed each other a few more times that day but I will never forget that first one. It had to be one of the best days of my life.

As I went home it was miraculous that I could even remember what my name was. I can remember getting home and sitting on the sofa with my parents and brother as they watched TV. I thought that I was gonna pop - if I could've called Phillippa right then I would've and probably could've talked to her for a week. That's how head over heels in love with her I was.

Let's get back to the kissing related stuff. Our relationship deepened over the next several months as we spent a lot of time together. One night I was at Phillippa's house and we were sitting on the sofa watching TV. It was totally dark in the room save for the TV set. Phillippa's mom (who is a great lady) walked in and said she had to go to the supermarket for a couple of minutes. Phillippa and I got to kissing each other after her mom left. It got fairly heated and Phillippa laid her head back on the arm of the sofa. I definitely did not want the kiss to stop so my head followed hers - the only problem was when her head rested against the sofa arm the impact caused her teeth to sink into my lower lip. I definitely did not notice it at that moment. I definitely did notice it the following morning!.

The following morning was a Sunday and we all got up to go to church. I was pretty tired from staying up so late the night before (remember, for a country kid like me staying up until eleven o'clock was a real feat). Tired or not I couldn't complain to my mother because then she would quickly tell me that if I got more rest I would have less problems getting up and going to church. Frankly, there was no way that I was gonna miss any time that I could spend with Phillippa. So I was up and standing by one of our space heaters reading the sports section of the newspaper. My mom asked me a question - in responding I dropped the newspaper down from my face. My mom said, "Edward, my God!" I wondered what in the world was causing her to say that? My mother then said, "I'll tell you what I'm talking about - just go take a look at your lower lip in the bathroom mirror!"

I went into the bathroom and looked at my lower lip - it had swollen up about three times the size of my upper one and was dark blue! I immediately thought about the sofa episode the night before. My mother (who thought the world of Phillippa) walked in and told me, "You ought to be ashamed! Ya'll must be trying to chew each other's faces off! You had better slow down some!" I promised her that we would. Then my mom added, "No way you can go to church with that. You'll have to stay home!" Given how tired I was between football practices and seeing Phillippa, staying home from church on a cold Sunday morning was not exactly a punishment. I stayed home and nursed the lip. (If by chance you're wondering what happened to Phillippa and me, she moved away several months later when her father was transferred to a church in Florida. Outside of my mother dying, this was the saddest event of my life. I truly cared for Phillippa - so much so that I was never to feel the same way about a girl again until I met my wife Debbie eight years later).

So I suffered my first kissing injury. There were to be more along the way. My senior year I dated a very nice girl named Jenny Gatliff (who was mentioned in the chapter one dog killing episode). Jenny was great and we dated off and on for five or six years. One thing that was a real plus about Jenny was the fact that she was a terrific kisser. She was pretty inventive, too. On one of my birthdays she gave me a certificate good for ten free kisses - I think I redeemed the whole thing on our next date. She also would buy these flavored lip glosses that she would allow me to try out. I got to where I encouraged her to buy them, not because I gave a damn about the flavored glosses but because I knew that the lip gloss = mucho kisses.

One time Jenny and I went to a church revival on a Saturday night. We went because she was one of the singers in the church choir. The revival ended about eight o'clock that evening. We then went back to Jenny's house, sat on her front porch swing, and must've kissed for the next three or so hours. We kissed so much that the next morning my lips were raw and my jaw muscles ached like hell! I did learn two useful things from this particular experience - Vaseline does work on raw lips and Ben-Gay helps sore jaw muscles too.

Going back yet again to my senior year in high school, I had the exhilarating experience of kissing three different girls in one day! Jenny, whom I just mentioned, went to high school during our first two class periods and then went over to Tift College for the rest of the day. She would leave right after the first break period which gave us the time to go smooch out in front of the auditorium (behind the columns to the entrance). Remember the story in chapter one when I talked about killing Jenny's dog? The girl that I mentioned there, Mary Jenkins, sort of dated me at the same time that I dated Jenny. Mary and I would get together after lunch in front of the entrance to our fifth period classes and engage in a brief smooch session before class began. Finally, a girl that I will always think a lot of, Kim Duckworth, got to be my riding-to-and-from-school-on-the-bus girlfriend. For a few magical days in 1974, I got to kiss all three of them each and every day! I was about as close to heaven as a seventeen-year old boy gets. Of course, for obvious reasons, this scenario couldn't (and didn't) last long but it was damn sure fun while it did.

Another senior year experience that I vividly remember occurred when I was going to a basketball pep rally early in 1974. At this point, because of what I mentioned earlier, I was dating neither Jenny, Mary, or Kim. Steven Davis, (a good friend of mine in high school) Ray, and I were sitting on the top row of bleachers watching the pep rally. I was minding my own business when there was a tug on my sleeve - I looked and it was a girl that I had never seen before. She looked me dead in the eye and said, "You're really cute. Can I kiss you?" I thought she was kidding and told her so. She said, "Is this kidding?" and laid one on me that caused my tonsils to do back flips. After the kiss I stammered, "God, that was great! Who are you?" She said, "My name is Laurie and I want some more." Ray, Steven, and I could hardly believe it.

The pep rally ended and the three of us walked back to class along with everyone else. In the midst of all these people, I felt another tug on my jacket. It was Laurie again. "I told you I wanted more!" With this, she threw her arms around me and kissed me in a way that reminded you of snakes writhing in the summer heat. If I remember right, we drew a fairly sizable crowd before I pulled away, afraid of expulsion from school (remember I'm two months from graduating) or some other similar punishment.

Thus far, I've told you about the good kisses. Don't get me wrong - there were plenty of bad ones too. I'll tell you about a few of those, but, because I'm a gentleman, real names will not be used.

WORST KISS EVER - In my senior year of high school, somewhere around April, I went out with this girl named Tammy. The date itself was okay until we got back to Tammy's house and started watching TV. One thing led to another and I ended up kissing her. As we kissed she sort of held her mouth wide open and did little else. It was like kissing an open hole or wind tunnel or something. One kiss like that was enough to last me for the entire evening. What made it worse though was that it seemed that the one kiss was not enough for her. She wanted to smooch some more. I got through it by figuring that if soldiers could endure the horrors of war that I could survive this situation. I did survive, but barely.

TOOTH KISSERS - Ever kissed someone that parted their lips but not their teeth? It's like kissing a cold steel knife or something. I've had one or two of these type kisses. It's like the initial expectation is good (parted lips) but then the rest is like a wax sandwich - you know you're getting something but there seems to be nothing to the something.

GROSSEST KISS - On another senior year date I had gone out with this girl that a couple of my friends said liked me. I picked her up the night of the date and let her in the passenger side of the car. By the time I had walked around and got in on my side she had slid over in the seat far enough that I had to make her move so that I would have room to drive. All the way to Macon she sat so close to me that I had to make her move each time I shifted gears! We went to this movie that was sort of romantic, which made the experience all the more worse. Ever been on one the those dates when after about the first five minutes you wished you'd stayed home? This was one of those type dates. To get to the kissing part, after about half an hour of the movie (I remember none of it because she kept whispering stuff in my right ear about how much fun she was having, that we would have to do this again, etc) there came a particularly romantic sequence. This girl looked me right in the eyes and said, "Let's do what we both want to do." With that statement she closed her eyes and leaned over towards me. Thinking this to be a casual kiss, I leaned over as well and met her lips halfway.

Instead of a casual kiss this girl's head picked up momentum as it came towards mine. The impact was somewhat like being tackled in football. Our heads bumped and our lips smashed together. The pressure was so great that it caused my lips to throb painfully. But this was not the worst part of it - after piledriving my lips this girl stuck her tongue all the way into the back of my mouth. I literally could not breath! I had to pull away due to the lack of breath and the pain. This girl though thought I was pulling away because, in her words, "...the passion is just so great. I know you're afraid of what you're feeling but I've held this in for so long. I don't care what we do but I want you!" With that, she launched another frontal assault on my bruised and bloody lips.

I managed to deflect this kiss by keeping my teeth tightly clenched. She pulled back and asked me why I wasn't responding to her? I made some kind of lame excuse about being attracted to her but not wanting to take advantage of her. Fortunately, she seemed to buy this but it also made her think more highly of me, which was not a good thing. I took her home and thought that no matter what happened I would never date this girl again. As it turned out, I never did, but later on I had to have an emotional discussion with her. In this discussion, I lied like crazy to her and said that I was afraid of getting too involved with her and that I had just gone through a relationship that had gone sour and blah blah blah........you can probably guess the rest.

SECOND GROSSEST KISS- One time in the early eighties I was working at a store in Sandy Springs, Atlanta. On one particular day the store was sponsoring a benefit for a local charity and had a kissing booth as part of the fund-raising events. A lady in the jewelry department and I were chosen as the female and male "kissees". The price was one dollar per kiss. This was an enjoyable experience for me until a lady from the office came up and gave me a dollar. She was probably in her fifties but was dressed like she was thirty. She plunked down the dollar and said, "I'm a-gettin' my dollars worth honey!" With that, she launched her oral attack. It was like a Ninja warrior competition taking place inside my mouth! The thrusts, jabs, and kicks were intense. It wasn't that her technique was so bad, it was just that this woman was older than my mother and was treating me in a very wanton fashion. For the first time in my life I began to understand why women complain of being treated as sex objects. I definitely felt like one after this experience.

Suffice it to say that these days my kissing expertise is limited to Debbie (the serious stuff) and the kids (the nice, Dad stuff). After that, that's about it. I have never been one of those types that likes to kiss and slobber all over people. I just don't like doing that. I think affection like that should only be shared by people that really care a lot about each other. And that's what I do - a much safer practice than what I followed in the days of my youth, I tell you for sure.

CHAPTER 7

BE UNIQUE/LIFE

All great authors at some point philosophize about their thoughts on the great mysteries of life. If it's good enough for them to do this, it's good enough for me. As in the rest of this book, there is no logical pattern or reason to what you're about to read.

1. No one ever achieved anything by being like someone else. It's truly amazing how many people want to follow the crowd. The funny thing is, all following the crowd gets you is membership in a faceless, nameless group. And its incredible that anyone would consciously choose this. I can remember being almost painfully shy until I was about twelve years old. I went to a church function and discovered that standing around in a corner watching your peers have a good time is not a lot of fun. I then noticed how one or two kids seemed to grab most of the attention. They were having the most fun of the entire group. It then hit me that these kids were popular because of either one of two things:

2. They were outgoing enough to attract attention to themselves. This fits nicely into the "follow-the-crowd" mentality. What outgoing people really do is give non-outgoing people a safe haven. They can be in the middle of something important or fun but not have to play a meaningful role in it. It's like auditioning for the school play and getting to be a part of the scenery. You're in the play but no one knows that you're there. What can be the fun of this type of

participation I don't know but apparently it appeals to a lot of people. It's this mentality that creates followers of all types - from those you see in most companies to the extreme cases like believers of religious cults. The only group that I truly associate with is the Brotherhood and, as I told you earlier, this group is comprised of rugged individualists.

3. They were involved in things that had status. It was for this reason that I played high school football. I enjoy sports but anyone that believes that getting the hell knocked out of you constitutes fun should have themselves committed to a psychiatric ward. Football was hell - it was also the most prestigious activity you could get involved in Forsyth, Georgia. That's why I played – football, it got you plenty of attention from the girls, free soft drinks at Castleberry's, permission to leave any class on game days and go to the gym to goof around, etc.

I can remember going with Jenny to a church hayride one Saturday night and being surrounded by kids who wanted to know about Friday night's game (which we won). Things like that really helped boost a young man's ego. It benefited me to teach myself to sing like Elvis - it got me invited to fraternity parties, nightclub talent contests, general parties, and other fun things. I could go into a club and sing one song that took a couple of minutes and get female attention for the rest of the evening. You didn't even have to try hard when you sang - women would walk over to the table and ask me to dance and stuff. Believe me - I am not trying to brag. It is merely an inescapable fact of life. Being different can enable you to grab the glory. In simpler terms, just remember this....

"Being different separates successful from non-successful people". Why did Elvis make it? Tom Edison, Billy Graham, or any of the others who have? Because they were like everyone else? No way – it's because they were different. You can have poor ideas or concepts and attract some notoriety if they're different. If I were a business school professor, I would teach courses in encouraging individuality, challenging the status quo, etc. Encouraging this ability would enable many to far exceed what life would typically hold out for them. We all have unique abilities that, if we weren't so damn shy about displaying them, could bring us accolades, success, and all the nice perks that go with it. Don't be afraid to do it! This book, for example, may never go anywhere but at least I took the shot! And if it never does anything, I tried, plus, I can at least print up a few copies for friends and relatives that will endure on a bookshelf somewhere long after I'm gone. Go for it!

4. There are damn few people that really care about you - cherish them and to hell with the others. I have found over time that as you move up the corporate ladder you attract lots of new "friends". These new "friends" will smile at you, call, invite you to events, etc. I still get amused that I can call people and say, "Hi, I'm Ed Williams from blankety-blank" and get instant service. Because of that tie-in I get invited to lunch, ball games, and other such things frequently. If I had a dime for all the protestations of friendship that I receive I'd be the Howard Hughes of Macon.

Just remember that many of these "friends" don't care a whit about you. Don't kid yourself - how many business colleagues do you think would spend any time with you 'if you lost your job? Damn few - that's how many! It's not you that they care about - it's the job or better put, what you can do for them. If you ever let yourself believe anything differently then you've made a big mistake. There is nothing wrong with business success and successful people should be proud of what they've done. But don't let success delude you - the job you hold is just a way to make a living - nothing more. Any time you allow it to define you or shape your identity as a person you have really screwed up.

I used to run around and try to do all these things with clubs/groups and it finally hit me - why? It has no impact on my job, plus, the time I spend with these people would be much better spent with Debbie and the kids or the Brotherhood. I've even had a couple of occasions where members of the opposite sex have expressed an interest in me - even though I'm married with two kids. Get real! Debbie married me when I was clerking at a store! There is no doubt in my mind that she married me for me - not for anything I represented, because at that time I represented nothing. But she cared for me as a person - with all my obvious flaws. That kind of affection and love could never be traded for some "Johnine come lately". But, it happens with lot of guys every day. I think they call these type women "trophy wives" or something. And it's amusing to observe it when some young woman is married to a successful old crock. It's easy to see what the deal really is - the guy's getting his ego fed because of the youth of the woman and the woman gets to live in a big house, spend money, and act like somebody. I'll end this diatribe with this thought - at some point in life, when your business career is over, the only people that are going to give a damn about you are your closest family members and friends. And you ought to determine who these people are now and give them your time and energy. It'll be the best and most fulfilling investment you will ever make.

5. Funerals stink! One of the things I've always wondered about is how the concept of funerals began - to me the entire process is ghastly. You start with a family that is grieving over the loss of a loved one. Then, you put them in a church with a zillion other people (many of whom don't half know the deceased). Finally, the topping of this ghastly sundae is the display of the remains of the deceased. The funeral service seems designed to ensure that even more grief be wrung out of the attendees. It just seems like the overall process is designed to emotionally wipe out the deceased person's survivors. If it were me, I would want to be buried immediately and not let anyone "view" me. I'd rather for the people that cared about me to remember me as I was, not as I would appear in that box. If condolences from loved ones are necessary, a small service comprised of people that were the closest to you would be sufficient. There is one thing for sure - you're not to going to know or care what's going on anyway at that point if you are the star of the festivities.

6. Gas emissions are eminently funny - at any occasion. As barbaric as funerals are, let someone attending break wind and you'll get a chuckle from almost everyone in attendance. This even includes the family of the bereaved! In fact, there is basically no situation whenever gas is passed that it doesn't result in a good bit of laughter. For some reason the sound, the knowledge of where the sound comes from, and the violation of the nostrils that occurs afterwards makes it funny. Ever notice a group of people in a room when someone has obviously cut the cheese? The people there may quietly grumble about it but they won't leave the room! In fact, you'll notice many of them surreptitiously inhaling the ill breeze in some sort of effort to grade it

("...worse than Uncle Fred's, equal to the mother-in-law's, etc.....").
Can you honestly say that you know of anyone that doesn't have a
good posterior fog story to tell? It's almost impossible to find anyone
that doesn't. I can remember in one of my previous jobs when the
group of managers I worked with decided to buy our boss two
Christmas gifts - one serious and one gag. The serious gift we bought
was an Atlanta Braves sweatshirt. The gag one was a remote-
controlled whoopee cushion. This is no joke - a remote controlled
whoopee cushion! It consisted of a small speaker and a remote. The
remote would work from as far as fifty feet away. We got both gifts
wrapped and ready for the upcoming Christmas party at my bosses'
house.

Soon came the night of the party. All of us at various times file in
with our wives and stand around the Christmas tree chatting. It's still
pretty formal at this point. Soon, Tim, the Plant Controller, comes in
with his wife and the two wrapped Christmas gifts. I asked Tim which
one was the "magic box?" Tim pointed to one of the boxes and said,
"Let me put both these under the tree, Ed."

Tim walks over and slips the two boxes underneath the tree. Now,
the tree happens to be situated pretty equidistant between the group
of wives, who are sitting on the sofa, and us guys, who are standing
around the bosses' pool table. Tim motions for me to come over and
talk with him. I walk over and he produces the remote for the whoopee
cushion! He then tells me, "Ed, we're gonna have fun tonight! I've
got the remote right here and when I wrapped that speaker, I made
sure not to put a top on the box. That way, when we hit this button,
those farts will sound ripe!"

I wanted to laugh like hell but managed somehow to choke it back.
The other managers mingled around and we began to discuss sports
and play some pool. I kept pestering Tim to use the remote to see
what would happen. Tim urged me to have patience until the time
was right to pull the trigger.

It became the right time a few minutes later when Brian, our
Production Manager, walked in. Brian had been out of town in
overseas meetings for the last week-and-a-half and didn't know about
the nature of our purchases. In fact, after a few minutes of small talk,
Brian said that he was going to walk over to the Christmas tree and

take a quick look at the gifts underneath. He proceeds to do this and kneels down next to the tree checking out the gifts. Quick as a flash, Tim sidles up and whispers, "Ed, the time is right." With this, he hits the button on the remote......

"BRAPPPPPPPP" went the speaker, sounding like twenty minutes past feeding time at a horse stable. I will never forget the look on Brian's face as long as I live - he stood up quickly and his face turned beet red. He quickly strolled over to where Tim and I were standing (our shoulders were bobbing up and down and we were vainly trying to hold back the laughter). I gathered my wits and then quickly said, "Damn Brian, what did you have for lunch?" Brian replied, "I didn't do that dammit! What are you sick shits up to?" Tim then cues Brian in on our little scheme. After hearing the details, Brian starts laughing and demands control of the remote.

Over the next twenty to thirty minutes Brian hits the button a few times. We saw a couple of interesting things happen - first, we found that the remote-controlled whoopee cushion had three different Bronx cheers programmed into it. There were a couple of short blasts and one long tuba concerto. Second, the guys all snickered and acted like idiots each time the speaker played its rump music. Oddly enough, the ladies present never seemed to notice these sounds even though I did see a couple of them look up after one or two of the more sonorous blasts.

After eating and socializing some more, we began opening the gifts. Our boss was delighted when he got to the remote-controlled whoopee cushion. First, he laughed heartily. Then, he took the remote upstairs and tested the cushion for distance. All of us guys must've hit the remote button five to ten times each while doing our own on-the-spot research. This experimentation went on for quite awhile and ended up creating such levity that this ended up being one of the best Christmas parties that I ever attended.

As a follow-up to this story our boss told us upon returning from Christmas shutdown that he had utilized the remote-controlled whoopee cushion on his father-in-law. Apparently this father-in-law had a bad habit of always sitting in my bosses' favorite chair when he visited. He then detailed the great delight he took in setting up the whoopee cushion speaker right underneath this chair. Then, his father-in-law visits and eventually plunks down in the chair. My boss then patiently waited until both his mother-in-law and wife entered the room. After a few minutes of conversation he eased out the remote and hit the button. This particular time the whoopee cushion peeled off the long tuba concerto blast. I laughed as my boss explained how the women sat upright in their chairs and his mother-in-law chastised her husband for farting in their children's home. I then asked my boss when he revealed the remote controlled whoopee cushion to his in-laws - he said that only after allowing his father-in-law to take a few more minutes of hard abuse. Apparently my bosses' wife and mother-in-law were really reading him the riot act for his crude behavior. Anyway, when the dust settled and my boss 'fessed up to the truth his father-in-law was so amused that he asked where he could buy his own electronic whoopee cushion? When told he could purchase one at Spencer's he called them and was told that they were sold out. Based on episodes like these I urge you to buy one of these new technology whoopee cushions should you ever see one. If you do I'll guarantee you that it will provide you raucous laughter for many years to come.

I have one other quick flatulence story that I just heard today. I laughed so hard at this story that I almost cried and nearly lost control of some of my bodily functions. It was told to me by Alan Woodrum and Cecil Asbell, two of my buddies.

Alan said last weekend that he was out at Macon Mall. A guy walked up to him out of the blue and said, "Remember me?" Alan said he vaguely recalled the face but had no idea as to who the guy was. The guy then said, "I'll give you a hint. Remember my name, Jeff Nitquartz!" Alan said he still didn't have a clue as to who the guy was. Then the guy said, "Remember—I'm the guy ya'll fired for farting over the PA system at the plant!" Thennnnn Alan recalled the guy!

It seems that a few years ago Jeff Nitquartz was a product technician at the plant. He worked on one of the two night shifts. One night Jeff had to get on the P.A. system and call for some raw materials for his line. For some unknown reason, right after he called for the raw materials Jeff held the microphone up to his rectum and emitted a loud blast over the PA system! By all accounts production was nearly shut down because the whole plant convulsed in laughter! At two o'clock in the morning! Cecil, who was the Production Manager of the plant at the time, was laughing so hard as Alan told this that I thought he was gonna cause himself to have some internal health problems.

After he calmed down, Cecil began talking about how he had to investigate this incident. Apparently he had to talk to Jeff and question him about what he had done. Cecil said that keeping a straight face throughout this meeting was hard enough, but, that he had to ask Jeff the question,

"Did you break wind over the PA system?" Cecil said that when he asked it that it took more self-control than he knew he had just to keep from laughing out loud! The real problem for Cecil occurred when Jeff answered,

"I just thought it was the thing to do! This damn plant is boring at night and I was trying to improve the morale!" When Jeff said that, Cecil said he lost control and busted out laughing! He then went on to say that after working in production for twenty-five years that this was the first time he had ever fired someone and laughed while doing it! And Jeff didn't blame him!

"I know it was wrong, but sometimes you have to get basic to get results!" he stated.

So, remember people. Simple pleasures are the best and laughing at wind emissions is one of those simple pleasures. Enjoy it when the cheese is squeezed - you'll be enjoying a pastime as old and revered as the human race itself.

7. I'm positive Will is my son. Before this even gets started, let me assure you that I know Will is my son. If I don't offer this disclaimer right up front, Debbie will have me out in the backyard sleeping in the hammock.

What I mean is, do you know how there are times when your child will do something that is obviously inherited from you? I just witnessed one of these times with Will.

My son, my dear ten year old son, walked up to me the other day and said he was hungry. Since he and I were alone (Deb and Alison were at the mall), I offered to take Will somewhere to feed him. When I asked him where he wanted to eat, he replied, "Hooters."

That's right. Hooters. My boy said he wanted to go eat at Hooters. It almost brought a tear to my eye. I knew right then that there could be no doubt as to his chromosome pool - the genes of Ed's Sr., Jr., and moi were flowing securely through his veins. It made me proud to know that the boy is a full-blooded, healthy, Williams male.

(Just in case you wondered, I didn't take him. He's still at that point in life where he confesses everything he does to his mother. And sure as hell, she'd never believe that it was Will that made the suggestion to go to Hooters. I'm slow, but I ain't crazy).

8. Can Arthur Whitley put the proper spin on a situation or what? Arthur Whitley is a good friend and co-worker of mine. He serves as the Maintenance General Foreman at my company. He is also as nice a guy as you would ever want to meet.

A few weeks ago at work we had a peace of equipment called a heat exchanger that just gave out. This heat exchanger has been in bad shape for years and is well-known among the guys as a candidate for the scrap heap.

Arthur was sent to go check on it and see if it could be repaired. This was a bad situation for him to be put in as budgets are tight right now, but, this heat exchanger needs to be junked and replaced with a new one. The only problem is that a new one would cost tens of thousands of dollars. We are not likely to be given that kind of money to spend right now, given the current business climate.

Arthur spent a couple of hours in the hot sun examining this heat exchanger. Try though he might, he could not come up with a way to fix it. When he returned to the maintenance office, he was approached by his boss and was asked about the condition of the heat exchanger. Arthur diplomatically replied, "It ain't in that bad a shape for the condition its in." When his boss pressed him as to what that statement meant, Arthur said, "What I mean is that it'll look good on the truck as it's hauled to the junk yard."

Doncha love the mesh of diplomacy, tact, and honesty Arthur uses? If I ever find myself on trial for committing a mass murder, I'll ask Arthur to be a character witness. With his oratorical skills, I'll probably be out on bail within weeks.....

9. Ever sign up for a "Win a free trip to Bermuda contest!" Every three or four years I'll forget and sign up for one of these trips - they

always seem to have sign-up forms for them at State Fairs and Dairy Queens. Anyway, you fill out one of these contest entry forms and lo and behold, in a week or so you get a phone call. You've won the contest! Now, all you have to do is drive down to Daytona Beach on a Wednesday to accept the prize. You also get to visit some time-share condos while you're there. The bad thing about this deal is that you know you've been had in the initial conversation when they call to tell you about your winnings. The only sure cure I've found when nailed with one of these calls is to pretend you're delighted to accept but that you have eight children to bring with you. For some reason, if these people think they've got to provide more than one motel room for the visit they back off. Obviously, the profit margin is thin in this scam if one extra motel room blows the whole deal. Save the time you spend on schemes like this and put it into more productive use, like distributing chain letters or something.

10. Accept the fact that women are smarter than men. Why do we men have so many problems accepting this? I haven't figured it out yet but it is inherently true. Why? They are a multitude of reasons women are smarter than men. First, most general IQ and aptitude-type testing promotes this belief. Secondly, ask yourself why....

You're nice to her relatives, even the dorky ones or the drunks or whatever.

You go to the mall. I cannot imagine any man with two testicles voluntarily submitting to a trip to the mall! It is akin to submitting voluntarily to a philosophy lecture in college. Men go to malls under duress - feminine induced duress.

We actually discuss things like window treatments, sashes, blinds, and stuff with them. There can not be a man in the world that really gives a damn about any of the above. I cannot imagine any circumstances that would cause me to care whether the blue chenille or red bal-dour or yellow canary ass curtains match with the molding in the room. It makes my brain absolutely explode to even think about such things. If you're a man and interested in these type things, go ahead and begin the hormonal treatments and surgery necessary to become the woman you've already become.

We mumble and stumble all over ourselves when they either express affection towards us or cry over some perceived wrong. I actually had a good friend of mine tell me that his wife cried because he looked at her funny! I thought he was kidding. Then he told me how he walked in on her during a sensitive scene in Forrest Gump. She looked up at him, he smiled, and she started crying. When he asked why, she said, "How anybody could laugh when Bubba is dead is beyond me! You're heartless!" My friend, in honest bewilderment, looked at me and asked, "How do you win?" I replied, "If I knew big man, I'd be famous and living in a house on the ocean." Go figure. The one I thing that I do know for sure is that when women cry, men will do anything to stop it. Anything. I know. I have.

I could list countless other reasons, but just go ahead and accept the fact that women are superior. They pull the strings. And we men are the Pinocchios of the world. We dangle by them, and choose to do so. If any woman ever decides to reveal how they intoxicate men into being so subservient, they could make a billion dollars because any guy I know would pay to understand how its done. The problem is, no woman will ever tell the secret. This would be breaking the "secret oath of womanhood" that I know they must all secretly take. The two things that are more important than money in this world are power and control. Women have both and thusly don't need the money. Although they have most of that too.

11. Don't call and ask Ray or Hugh or I to join the Brotherhood. You can't. Don't even think about it. Join something easier to get into, like the White House Staff or the management of Fort Knox.

12. The Singapore Caning. Remember a while back when the big deal was made out of the teenager who got caned in Singapore for vandalism? It was all over the newspapers and TV and even President Clinton urged the Singapore government not to carry the punishment out.

I wondered what the big deal was about a basic asswhupping. Hell, for me and a lot of other Southern boys getting one's ass occasionally scorched was just part of the growing-up experience.

As the controversy around this episode went on, I discovered some interesting things....

13. The kid that was caned had a questionable history. Was in and out of trouble over the last two to three years with several minor scrapes with the law. He wasn't a terrible kid, but, did seem to get into a lot of petty problems of one sort or the other. He appeared to be your typical smart-ass, rich-kid type that probably needed his ass blistered.

14. When they whip your ass in Singapore they really whip your ass. Apparently they use some kind of cane rod that is soaked in water for a period of time before the asswhuppin' is administered. It has flanges and stuff sticking out of it that can (and do) draw blood from the recipient. The blows hurt so badly that some who have experienced it have had their asses bleed and even have passed out from the pain. The punishment is so intense that the number of lashes to be administered are seriously discussed by the Singapore judicial system. It is an obviously an asswhupping to be remembered.

A funny thing happened though - as accounts of the upcoming ass frying became known, the American public generally supported the caning. I guess after all these years of vandalism and teen-age crime run amuck that we got a vicarious thrill out of seeing a snobby rich kid getting his ass filleted. I have to admit that I got a laugh out of the situation and was glad that the kid's ass got converted into hamburger meat.

I know some of you out there are probably thinking about how heartless I am after reading that. The only thing I can counter with is this - has the kid gotten into any other trouble since the caning? I haven't heard of any.

15. Never eat three Nu-Way hot dogs, a large order of fries, and drink a large Diet-Coke at 9:30 p.m.! I did this, and lived to tell the story...

A few years ago, I had to work real late one night. It also happened that on that particular night Debbie and the kids were spending a few days with Debbie's parents. I was starving and decided to grab something from a fast food joint on the way home.

Before going any further with this, I have to tell those of you among the uninitiated about Nu-Way hot dogs. They are among the greatest delicacies that have ever existed. In the 1930's a Greek immigrant started up a hot dog stand in downtown Macon. He served a red-dye frank with unions, Greek chili, and mustard. These hot dogs were very good and quickly caught on. Pretty soon, thousands of Maconites and other mid-staters were scarfing down tons of these hot dogs.

The original Nu-Way site in Macon still exists (I read an article where they have had to replace the floor four times because the numbers of customers literally wore it out) along with eight or nine others. These hot dogs are the greatest I have ever tasted! Noted author Lewis Grizzard ate them by the truck load. The word was that when he was passing through he would buy a gross of them and take them back home to Athens and put 'em in his freezer. These hot dogs are so good that I feel like I've taken a sedative after my usual Nu-Way meal (three hot dogs all the way, large order of fries, and a large Diet Coke). I have to have them at least once each couple of weeks. Alan Woodrum, Cecil Asbell (aforementioned friends) and I use to head to Warner Robins once or twice a week to get what we termed "our fix." These hot dogs are that good. Health food fanatics hate them, which is also another reason we eat them. You see, fitness fanatics have it all wrong. Their theory is that if they exercise, take vitamins, and watch what they eat that they'll live to be a hundred. Perhaps they will, but, why would you want to if it means eating alfalfa sprouts and tofu? Personally, I would rather live to be forty (one year from now as I write this) and eat what I want to instead of living like an emaciated German monk.

My theory on longevity is that if you eat all this healthy stuff, sooner or later you'll get in a situation where you have to eat a little grease or cholesterol. You'll be in a pinch somewhere, extremely hungry, and grease and cholesterol laden foods are all that are available. You then eat some "tainted" food and guess what? Your system can't take it! It's been so shielded from the real world that it goes on overload and before you know it you're dead. This is real sad when it happens - a healthy dead person. I went to a funeral for a healthy dead person one time. I looked in the casket and thought about how many times old Jim had told me about the benefits of a healthful diet and of healthful living. And what did it get Jim? A heart attack from excessive exercise! And for what - depriving yourself of a normal life? What a joke!

The Ed Williams theory says that you should occasionally load up on high cholesterol, high-caloric type foods. The reason for this is very simple. Notice how people that continually handle venomous snakes, like rattlesnakes and stuff, develop an immunity to the poisons? In fact, after some period of time they can take a bite from the most venomous snake around and never feel a thing. That's because they've built up an immunity that protects them from the poison. Well folks, food is the same way. I think that if you go in, hit the fries and hamburgers on occasion (I love good ice cream too, especially Breyer's butter pecan), that you'll develop immunities to fat, sugar, and cholesterol! After doing that, you can eat pretty much what you want for the rest of your life! In fact, if this book makes it, my follow-up should be a cookbook for those of you that want to follow the healthy, good for you, Ed Williams high fat and cholesterol laden diet. Remember this - I'm still alive and in fairly decent shape. I can still sing an Elvis song, enjoy a good movie, good times with good friends (the Brotherhood), and play with my kids. There are many healthy dead people out there that can't say this. You may scoff but remember, they laughed at Edison and Einstein too.

Anyway, back to the hot dog story. I was going home from work and dying of hunger. Lo' and behold, I spotted the Northside Drive Nu-Way! Instantly, my mouth was watering. I pulled purposefully into the drive-through and placed the order. I took the sweet smelling bag of treasures home, poured them out on a plate (for some reason, I hate to eat off paper plates), and devoured them in about fifteen minutes. Then, I took a shower, brushed my teeth, and hit the sack.

I woke up the following morning literally bathed in sweat. I was breathing hard and wondering just what in the hell was going on? As the fog cleared from my head, I started remembering that I had just experienced one of the strangest dreams I'd ever had in my life. The memory of this dream started coming back to me....

I dreamed that I was in a huge church and was all dressed up in a tux and about to get married. The church must've had two hundred rows of pews - it was that big. I was standing around, all dudded up, and having casual conversations with some of the onlookers in row two. None of my relatives or friends were anywhere to be found in this church (a fact that is probably good given the direction that this dream took). I talked for awhile with the row two inhabitants and then, suddenly, trumpets started going off. This told me that the ceremony was about to begin.

I took my position up front with my best man, whom I neither knew nor had the foggiest idea of who he might be! We waited up there and suddenly ten rows of flower girls walked out. They were throwing petals everywhere. Behind them came the bride's father. It is good he came out as I did not have the foggiest idea as to who my bride-to-be was and figured he might be able to shed some light on it. Anyway, the father came up and planted himself to my left. From way in the back of the church I began to discern my bride-to-be as she began walking down the aisle....

As she came up the aisle, she took a step and paused, then took a step and paused. Damn, will she ever get to the front of the church? As she continues to move closer, I notice that she is blonde, slender, about five foot five, and is actually quite attractive. I also notice that I still don't have a clue as to who she is and why I'm marrying her. To clear this up, I walk over from my position and begin talking to the stranger I was conversing with earlier on row two. I pose the age old question, "If it was you, would you marry her?" "No way", the row two stranger said. I thanked him and retook my position.

The minister started reading through the ceremony. My mind was racing - why am I doing this? Do I know her? The minister asks my bride-to-be if she will be my lawfully wedded wife? She replies in a clear voice, "Yes, I will. " The minister then asks me if I will take her to be my lawfully wedded wife? I say, in an equally clear voice, "No sir, I sure don't."

With this, my bride-was-to-be drops her head and takes a seat on the front pew. She is consoled by yet more people that I do not know. Suddenly, an old battle ax from row three jumps up, rushes towards my bride was-to-be, and says, "I knew you would never get married!" (I found out later when the cops came that this woman was my mother-in-law-to-be). With this, she clasps her hands around my ex-wife-to-be's neck and starts choking her. At this point the cops rush in and grabs the mother-in-law and the daughter (I never knew how much damage was inflicted upon my bride-to-be) and hauls them out of the church. Understandably, I am standing there somewhat in a state of shock. I guess the strangling of the wife you didn't and never knew can do that to a man. The shock wore off though when a familiar cry rang out through the church.....

"Welllllllllllllll, dogies!" It was Jed Clampett from the Beverly Hillbillies!. Along with him were Granny, Jethro, and Elly Mae. Uncle Jed reminded me that it was time to get in the truck and go home for vittles. I told him that I would and followed the Beverly Hillbillies out of the church. I got into the truck and, in a gesture I considered an honor, got to ride up top in the sofa that Granny sat in! The last thing I remember about this dream was Granny saying, "She was too damn skinny anyway! Yer better off, boy!"

Now after a dream like this I resolved that my nocturnal eating habits had to change. From this point forward I swore never to eat a Nu-Way hot-dog after normal lunchtime hours. This way, the calming-after-lunch effect would be invoked whenever I wanted it but the nocturnal, LSD dream-type effect would be avoided. Nu-Way fans though, do not take alarm - I will eat them until the day I die. I just won't eat them late at night unless I need to get legally high for some reason. I'm afraid that if I eat a bunch of them again late in the evening that Freddie Krueger will show up in my dreams or something. Anyway, be sure if you ever come through Macon that you have a Nu-Way. You'll be glad you thought to do it.

16. Women and men are never in synch as to when they want to have sex. I dearly love my wife Debbie - wouldn't trade her for all the money in the world. We have a great sex life but there is one thing I've noticed. If I have a day where everything goes smooth, no major problems, and come home full of vim and vigor I can't get her to look at me. But, let me work a twenty-hour day (and feel like someone has taken a giant syringe and sucked the life out of me) and I can't beat her off with a stick! This must be nature's way of seeing that none of us ever goes overboard regarding sex. (Of course, I'm convinced at this point that if women had the attitudes about sex that men do that none of us would ever leave the house). Anyway, just come home and act all whipped out and you will get laid - works every time!

17. Daughters are phone sharks. For some reason that I don't yet

understand, my daughter Alison has an irresistible urge to pick up a ringing telephone. And not just pick it up. When Alison is in the house she will not let the phone ring more than once before answering it. It is for this reason that I have dubbed her the phone shark. She doesn't just answer the phone, she pounces on it! Debbie tells me she will jump over chairs, dodge furniture, and sidestep the refrigerator to make it to a ringing phone. This is in contrast to myself, who would junk every phone in the house if I could. Alison and the phone - the perfect marriage. (As a side note she has already, at age twelve, requested her own cellular phone. I would probably have to sell drugs to be able to make the monthly payments she would run up on it.)

18. You know you're getting old when all the records you like are in the discount bin at the record store. Okay, it's the CD store now. And yes, I own a bunch of CD's. But "records" is still how I like to think of them.

I'll admit that my musical tastes begin with 1956 and end in the early eighties (I say the early eighties because the Bangles came along then and I liked them a lot). Other than that period of time, I pretty much disregard current music. It's not that I dislike rock'n'roll - I love it! It's just that during the period I mentioned, people actually played and sang their own music. And it was very good. Today, most of the groups are "enhanced" in the studio to the point that some of them cannot go on tour because they are not capable enough musically to perform in front of crowds. I stay with the oldies - period.

One thing I notice now when I go to the record stores is that all the good stuff is in the discount rack. I've made comments like, "Can you believe the Guess Who for $5.99? It must be a mistake!" or "Three Dog Night - it's a steal at $3.99!" You label yourself within a certain age bracket by hanging around the discount racks. The clerks in the stores (they always seem to be about sixteen) will sort of look at you and laugh as you search around looking for old musical treasures.

A couple of years ago it was getting close to Christmas and Debbie asked me what I wanted. I don't know why, but the one thing that hit me was that I wanted a Bachman-Turner Overdrive video. I figured the band was surely taped in concert at some point and that if you looked hard enough a video could be found. I explained all this to Debbie and she agreed that she would go to Blockbuster and see if they had a Bachman-Turner Overdrive video.

Debbie said she walked in one weekday morning to inquire about the video. The clerk in the store appeared to be an age sixteen (or so) female. Deb walks up and asks her if she can order a tape? The clerk very promptly pulls out a large catalogue and asks Debbie what type tape she wants? Debbie explains that she wants a tape featuring Bachman-Turner Overdrive. The clerk nods and starts thumbing through the large catalogue. She looks and looks and looks - finally, after a couple of minutes, this clerk looks up at Debbie and says, "I'm sorry, mam (usage of this word is a definite giveaway that you're getting old) - I can't find anything by them but we do have a large classical music collection!" What a shot between the eyes! An unmistakable sign that we're both getting long in the tooth. I won't make any other comments regarding this subject other than if you happen to be reading this and work for Blockbuster, take note. Be sure and put a clerk in your stores in his/her late thirties/early forties that can speak the same language as the rest of us baby boomers. You'll probably do great business if we know we can ask for Grand Funk Railroad and receive a knowing smile from the person across the counter.

19. Buying prophylactics after you've been married awhile is an embarrassing business. When Debbie and I decided to have the Will (Will sometimes refers to himself as "the Will"), her doctor instructed us to get her off her birth control pills. The only difficulty in this is that when you go off the pill you have to utilize "alternative birth control methods" until the birth control pill hormones or fertilizer or whatever migrates out of the woman's system. Well, for a man, alternative birth control methods can only mean one thing.

The good, old fashioned prophylactic (or rubber, as I was instructed to call them by many peers and even Ed Jr.). I mean, generally what other birth control choices are there? Diaphragms? They remind you of the infield tarp at Atlanta Stadium. Plus, the chances of procreation taking place using these things are much greater than what I'm comfortable with. Foams and jellies? Wow, these are great passion promoters. Just before the moment of truth, you hear the gentle sighs of, "Stop while I insert the applicator." Having sex using that stuff is like trying to simultaneously take a shave and eat jello. The rhythm method? It seems that a lot of couples who've tried this method ultimately are listening to the rhythm of a rocking cradle. Abstinence? Get real, I ain't dead yet. So, rubbers it has to be.

You know, when you're a thirty-year old man who has already been married five years you think that your rubber buying days are over. The only thing more embarrassing than buying a rubber at that point is having to buy feminine hygiene devices for your wife. I can remember thinking that maybe I could just last out the pregnancy by swearing off sex for a few months. What a stupid idea that was! I'm one of those people that needs sex on a pretty frequent basis. I can remember that after a few days of the abstinence strategy I was beginning to find Captain Kangeroo appealing. Given this disgusting set of circumstances, the only thing to do was buy the damn rubbers.

I can remember thinking up a strategy for the purchase. I'm serious - a strategy. I felt that the humiliation potential in this situation was huge. So huge that the act of purchasing these things had to be well thought out in advance and a plan devised.

My first thought was simply to get Debbie to buy them. This was accepted like a smitty on a hearse. "If I can have the baby you can at least do this!" Well, what else are you gonna do? Give up sex and watch a lot of three AM television? No way, as I told you earlier. I've already seen more Abdominizer infomercials than I ever wanted to anyway. I had to step up to the plate and buy these rubbers.

We put our plan into effect one Saturday afternoon. For those of you who are faced with this situation in the future, I went out and cased a lot of department and discount stores and found that the best place to purchase rubbers is a certain large discount retailer (which I'll call X-Mart)! The reasons for this are:

1. They stick their pharmacies way over in the corners of their stores. This is really smart when you think about it. Do you want to be out in the open when purchasing hemorrhoid ointments, corn/callus removers, or Dr. Sholes foot pads? I mean, nothing could be worse. Think about having these type goods in your cart, or, worse yet, be in the act of examining the package and a friend or relative walks up. You might as well admit to cross-dressing as it would be less embarrassing.

2. Big rubber selections - not only do they have all the standard

name brands, they also carry ribbed lambskins (that are big enough to hold a ball-peen hammer, much less your puny little protruder) and colored and/or flavored prophylactics. I truly believe that one of the reasons X-Mart isn't totally out of business is because of their prophylactic sales. In fact, if X-Mart were really smart, they'd capitalize on this strength and establish prophylactic boutiques and occasional prophylactic fashion shows. I mean, getting models for these fashion shows would be a breeze if the same principles were employed that are used with fashion models for clothing. What I mean is, do you ever notice when they get fashion models for clothing that they are always emaciated, undersized women? Since there are plenty of men with emaciated, undersized organs there should be no problem in getting all the models ever needed for prophylactic modeling. (If the people at X-Mart are reading this they should at least send me a few bucks when these ideas catch on and you double prophylactic sales in your stores).

3. Mostly ugly women shop at X-Mart. This is important to know for a male about to purchase prophylactics. As embarrassing as it is to get caught by a pretty woman when examining or purchasing them, there should be no qualms at all about letting ugly women watch you buy them. I think the psychological reasoning behind this is that ugly women typically don't know much about sex (since they seldom experience it except if they frequent bars that are promoting "three for one" happy hour specials), so there is no reason to be embarrassed. They probably think you're purchasing gourmet balloons or something.

Debbie and I entered the store around two in the afternoon. Debbie was there as part of the agreement we had made regarding the purchase (her role in this situation will become clearer as the story continues) of these rubbers. When we got there I followed standard routine procedures that all adult males use when purchasing prophylactics. First off, when you enter the store you don't make a mad dash right over to where they are. You just sort of casually wander around and then ease over to where they're located. Using these time-tested strategies, we slowly worked our way over to the rubbers rack. Debbie positioned herself at an angle so that I would be forewarned if someone we knew walked up. Let's face it - with the luck I have my preacher or grandfather or someone would happen by while I was in the act. If this happened, it would not be just be embarrassing, it would be a psychological nuclear implosion of immense magnitude! To avoid a catastrophe like this, Debbie stood watch.

Once thing I was sure of while gazing at the racks was that I did not want to have to buy another box of rubbers anytime in the near future. With this thought in mind I looked for large quantity boxes, boxes with enough rubbers in them that years could go by without me using them all up. I noticed that the good people at the @#%&* Company had a box of thirty-six fun inhibitors, so, I grabbed them up. Immediately following this Debbie and I proceed to the check-outs.

It is critical when making a prophylactics purchase to scope out the people on duty at the front cash registers. The ideal cashier for a rubbers purchase is a female around the age of seventeen or eighteen. The reason this is true is that X-Mart cashiers are somewhat promiscuous and the purchase of rubbers doesn't even phase them. In fact with their experience, they can give you useful recommendations as to what brands to use and when sales on them might occur. Might as well save a few bucks if you can. Cashiers you don't want to utilize are those that are entering their golden years. Don't get me wrong - I have nothing against older people, in fact, I'm working on getting old myself. The problem that you have with older cashiers is that you're taking an eyesight risk. What I mean by this is that you don't want to plop the box of rubbers down on the check-out table and have the cashier hold up them up (for everyone to see) and state, "Can't quite make out the price on these Madge", as she holds them aloft for another cashier to ogle. (Older cashiers seem to always turn out to be the department head of your Sunday school group who's working a part-time job to make extra money on the weekend). So, for these reasons, its vital to get a seventeen or eighteen year old cashier.

With the selection criteria established, we walked into the front check-out area to select a cashier. After surveying the possibilities we noticed a seventeen or eighteen year old cashier working down the way. She was the one! Debbie and I strolled resolutely towards her check-out line.

When we first saw this cashier she had one or two people in line. But, I found that once you get in a line with a box of rubbers, twenty more people will join you. This is one of the by-laws of rubber purchasing and it ensures that your selection will be seen by as wide a viewing audience as possible.

It seems like we stood in that damn line for two years. Such is life during times of stress. We had even devised a plan for how we would stand in line. Debbie stood behind me so that when we got up to the register she could stand at an angle and block off the view to those in line behind us (at this point about one hundred and ten people). More time passed by and finally we got to the front of the line.

I took out the other items we were purchasing first and laid them on the check-out counter in order to create a little diversion. Then, after glancing over at Debbie to be sure that she was shielding the crowd properly, I took out the box of prophylactics and laid them on the counter as well.

Our seventeen-or-so year old cash register operator looked at me and said, "Looks like a good weekend for you!" and smiled. I mumbled, "It will be when this is over." With that, she smiled again, calmly rung up the purchase, and plopped the rubbers into a bag. It was so seamless that only one seventy-plus year old lady behind us even arched an eyebrow. I felt an overwhelming sense of relief and accomplishment when the cashier gave me my receipt and change. I strolled out of the store resolutely with pride and renewed vigor.

As we drove home the thought hit me again about having to buy more of these things. After all, a box of thirty-six penis protectors will not last forever. Alas, twas not to worry! As I discovered in the ensuing months, the importance of my penis in Debbie's life dropped significantly as she got more and more pregnant - almost like a record that starts out in the top five but vanishes off the charts after a short time. I guess that since your penis is blamed for the morning sickness, the swelling of the stomach, and all the other goodies that go along with pregnancy, that it is only appropriate that it should be forgotten and abandoned as the impending birth approaches. Anyway, as it turned out, this episode was to be the last of its kind in our lives.

We had already predetermined that we would have two children regardless of what their sexes turned out to be. We had also determined that after the second child (Will) was born that I would get a vasectomy. This event in and of itself is the subject of a future chapter as it was one of the most traumatic experiences in my life. So, in closing this, the best advice I can give you about purchasing rubbers is to follow the simple steps mentioned earlier. That should assure that you have as painless an experience as one can possibly have. Also, you should always remember to thank your local X-Mart management for the service they provide us all with as regards the outstanding rubber inventories they maintain in their stores.

4. If you don't know what a Yoo-Hoo is, you can't be a true Southerner! There's nothing better before, during, or after the Nu-Way experience than to guzzle down a Yoo-Hoo. Now, I'm sure many of you Northerners out there don't have a clue as to what I'm talking about. And that's as it should be. After all, most true gourmet experiences emanate from the South. And that's as it should be as well. Just remember that when you get south of Graceland (the real north-South divider) to pull up at any convenience store and ask for a Yoo-Hoo. If you don't like it, write me in care of my publisher as I would love to hear your story. Suffice it to say, other than Elvis CD's and Forrest Gump, there are few things better.

5. NEVER let Ron Miller purchase concessions for you at an Atlanta Braves game! Ron Miller and I worked together for a couple of years. You will read more about Ron and his extensive knowledge of jock itch in an upcoming chapter. Right now, what's important is that Ron was/is a good friend of mine. The story now continues......

About a year or so ago I got some tickets to an Atlanta Braves game. I invited Ron and a couple of other friends to go along. We were all just sitting there enjoying the game when I began noticing all the vendors hawking peanuts, popcorn, beer, etc. I was beginning to get pretty hungry.

I decided I wanted a bag of roasted peanuts. It galled me as I noticed the stadium vendors had badges on saying that the damn things cost three dollars! It's getting where families soon will have to take out another mortgage on the house in order to have the finances necessary to afford a night at the ballpark. Anyway, Ron is sitting on an aisle seat and I asked him if he would buy me a bag? Ron said sure and I slipped him a ten to pay for it. Sure enough, after a few minutes a vendor walks by our aisle and Ron gets the peanuts. He passes the bag over to me along with three dollars.

"Three dollars? Damn, I thought those peanuts were three bucks!" I exclaimed. Ron said, "They are three dollars but I guess I made a mistake. Anyway, you'll enjoy them more knowing that you paid seven dollars for them." Then he started laughing like hell about it! I said something else about the peanuts and Ron said, "Are you here to watch the ballgame or debate economics? Personally, I'm here to watch the ballgame."

I couldn't debate that logic. Just suffice it to say that Ron is a fine man and fun to do stuff with, but, a mathematics professor he ain't.

6. If you must marry, marry a rich orphan. Let me qualify this remark by making the appropriate self-serving, hen-pecked statement that I am quite pleased with my spousal choice. This is advice I got from Ed Jr. many, many years ago. It is fundamentally sound so I thought that I would pass it along to you.

7. I love the ole' Killer. . . How can anyone not love the ole' Killer, Jerry Lee Lewis? I sure do and I'll tell you why.

When I was two years old, my mother wrote in my baby book that I learned to operate her record player. And the one record that I played over and over and over was the classic Jerry Lee hit, "Great Balls Of Fire." How could anyone not like this song? It has a beat to it that would make you tap your feet at a funeral home. In fact, my mom said that I played it so much that she finally grew sick of the song.

I've also admired how the Killer takes responsibility for the decisions he has made in life. We may not like all of them, or agree with them, but he is not a hypocrite - he bears the responsibility for his choices. And how can you dislike a guy that would tell a whole church full of people, "Well if I'm goin' to hell - I'm goin' there playin' the piano." You can't.

One of the most touching parts of my life came a few weeks ago when I saw the ol' Killer on television. He was appearing at the Grand Ole' Opry and was asked by the host of the show to play the first song that he ever remembered playing in front of an audience. Jerry Lee sang and played, "The Old Rugged Cross." There wasn't a dry eye in the house when he finished. Nor was there in front of my television set.

I thank God for Jerry Lee Lewis. He is the most talented rock'n'roll musician ever. And I think a much better man than people give him credit for being.

8. People put down pro wrestling- but bring it up in a conversation....

Try this out sometime - go to a party or something and get into a group conversation. Generally the topics discussed will be pretty predictable - business, the weather, OJ, politics, or something like that. Go along with the conversation for awhile, then, in your best "don't give a damn" voice say, "Did you see Ric Flair on NITRO last night? Man, that was a great exhibition he put on." Then ease back and watch....

A few members of the group will look puzzled, one or two may even look annoyed, but inevitably someone will say, "Yeah, he put on a good show, didn't he?" You respond and before you know it, one or two more will make comments like, "That Hulk Hogan's big, isn't he?" Or "Does Roddy Piper still wrestle?" Or whatever.

The fact is that millions of people watch pro wrestling. And if you take it for what it is, sports entertainment, it can be very fun to watch. The interviews to me are the best part. Some of these guys, especially Ric Flair, do a tremendous job of hyping matches with future opponents. They make it sound as if the future of western civilization rides on the outcome. In fact, they do this so well that the World Wrestling Federation, one of the two big wrestling organizations, grossed around five hundred fifty million dollars in 1992 (I remember this from a group presentation that was done in a marketing course I taught several years ago). Three hundred million dollars of that total came from merchandising! Anyway you look at it, it's a huge business that continues to grow.

Let's get back to the party conversation topic. As you attend these functions, you'll note that some people typically do not 'fess up to watching wrestling. I guess they feel it demeans their image or something. Never mind that millions of us openly paid our money to watch the Batman movies, which essentially details the escapades of a grown man dressed in purple underwear, wearing a bat mask, and fighting bizarre criminal characters with high-tech gadgets. Think about it for a second - I liked the Batman movies, but, you have to admit that the basic premise is pretty ridiculous.

In this context I have no trouble bringing up the subject of wrestling in an open conversation. And, it happens every time, someone will admit watching and before you know it you can get a pretty decent conversation going. Try it and see - you'll find that not only can you get a pretty good chat going but you can once again marvel at yet another of the marvelous quirks of human nature.

9. Why do they give you sherbet at these fancy restaurants to "cleanse your palate" before they bring the real food out? I've had the opportunity to go to a couple of really nice restaurants where they engage in this practice. The gist of it is, after you finish your salad, the waiter walks out with a tiny bowl of sherbet. The first time this happened to me I thought they were trying to stiff me on the entree and go right on to the desert. When I tried to tactfully ask where the real food was, I was told that the sherbet was to "prepare my palate" for the upcoming meal. Prepare the palate - what in the hell does that mean? Does it mean they want your tongue numb in anticipation of what they're gonna bring out for you to eat? I don't understand this at all - if anyone out there does, please send me a note or call me so that I can be enlightened.

10. You know beef stew is good when.... My grandmother on Ed Jr.'s side, Miss Lily, used to make beef stew that was so good that I would ask for it as a birthday present! I'm deathly serious - she would make a big kettle of it and add a side order of her biscuits (which alone were enough to kill for) and give them to me for my birthdays. The broth in the stew was light but very tasty and I fondly remember its sumptuous taste. Even if someone else has the recipe now (which I'm sure somebody in the family does) I wouldn't want any as I don't want to dilute the memories I have of Miss Lily's stew. She was one of the best people I have ever known in my life.

11. The word "ass" can be a unit of measurement. One thing that I always get a chuckle out of is how Ed Jr. uses the word "ass" as a unit of measurement. I'll give you a quick example - my dad , as we were growing up, made a habit out of growing a large vegetable garden each year. He always grew it behind our house at the bottom of the hill that we lived on. Anyway, one day I remember Ed Jr. coming into the house after going to pull some ears of corn. Apparently, there was

a lot of corn down there cause as he came into the back yard he said, "Damn, it's hot. There must be an ass of corn down there!"

"An ass of corn, Dad?" I asked.

"Yeah", he said seriously, "an ass of corn."

I burst out laughing and he had this honest look of bewilderment on his face. It was like, why would you question this? He then explained to me that a large quantity of anything was considered an "ass". Then he looked at me like I was touched and said, "Don't show your ignorance."

And that's why you should always refer to large amounts of anything as an ass of whatever it is. For God's sake, don't show your ignorance.......

12. If you really need rain, hang a snake in a tree. I know this sounds crazy but it is one of those old country myths that got started somewhere long ago in these parts. Rightly where, I don't know.....

My first contact with this practice came when I was about twelve years old. We had had a real hot summer in 1968. It was sometime in early August and it had not rained in weeks. Our grass and vegetable gardens were dying, the ponds in the area were drying up, and it was just generally drier than I could ever remember it being. Ed Jr., perspiring heavily one day while cutting the grass, walked up to my brother and I and said, "Dammit, I may need to hang up a snake." My brother and I looked up and said, "What? Hang up a snake?" Ed Jr. then told us that it was a scientific fact that if a drought was going on that the only way it could be broken was to kill a snake and hang it off a tree limb. Of course, my brother and I thought that Ed Jr. was kidding but he was dead serious. We pondered this new found scientific knowledge for a while and then Brother and I went back to whatever we were doing and Ed Jr. continued cutting grass.

We didn't really think much more about the snake thing until one afternoon we saw our dad carrying a large, dead snake across the backyard. Brother and I ran outside and asked Ed Jr. what was he doing? Ed Jr. stated, "I told ya'll the other day that we needed to hang up a snake. Seen any rain lately?" We both had to admit that we had not. Ed Jr. then enlightened us that nothing ever really gets done unless people take action and that he was a man of action. He then walked over to a large oak tree, tied a piece of rope around the snake's neck, and hung him from the limb of the tree.

Brother and I laughed at the ole' man and ridiculed his snake hanging theory. Ed Jr. just looked at us and said, "Okay, we'll see how this all works out." Brother and I reiterated that we thought he had lost his mind and then we went on about our business.

Around midnight that evening I awoke to the sounds of a thunderstorm . It was so strong that you could hear the rain beating against the roof. As soon as I got out of the blither of being half-asleep I realized that I was hearing the first rainfall that we had had in weeks. Very quickly I woke my brother up so he could hear it too (he really appreciated me doing that). We both discussed whether or not the snake thing had anything to do with the rain. Ed Jr. then walked in our room and said, "Damn right it did!"

Brother and I listened the next day to weather reports that talked about how suddenly this storm system had sprung up and how none of the weather professionals had seen it coming. Of course, Ed Jr. seized upon this to reinforce his snake-hanging theory as the causal factor. You couldn't help but wonder about it but Brother and I wouldn't dare support the old man's theory. We wrote it off as happenstance and continued our day-to-day activities.

A few years later another drought hit our area. Weeks and weeks went by with no rain. Ed Jr. got that same serious look going and soon was seen dragging the carcass of another chicken snake across the backyard. Our dad got the requisite piece of rope and hung him up in the same tree that he had before. My brother and I laughed heartily again at this and teased Ed Jr. about it.....

That afternoon, the sky darkened. Soon thereafter, the bottom fell out of the clouds and rain once again pelted the ground. Sheets of rain came down - Ed Jr. walked up to my brother and I and said, "Well?" At this point, we laughed but we also really wondered about Ed Jr.'s snake hanging theory. A dead snake hung up in a tree brings rain?

Over the years our dad hung up another snake or two during times of drought. And damned if every time he had did, rain fell soon after!

You know, I really should sell the secret of snake hanging in a seminar or something, but, in order to help mankind I am revealing it here. A few things need to be clarified at this point though:

1. Only non-poisonous snakes should be used. Ed Jr. swears that a poisonous one will not work.

2. You leave the snake in the tree until the rain comes. In the time I saw Ed Jr. do this, it never took more than one or two days for the rain to come after the hanging of the snake.

3. Once the rain has fallen the snake should be cut down from the tree and disposed of. If you continue to leave it up you'll get more rain but it won't work for you in the future as you will have abused the power.

Ya'll can all laugh but damned if it didn't work whenever Ed Jr. did it........

4. The Atlanta Braves were the World Champions of baseball! God it's good to say it! The Braves were the World Champions. This may not mean anything to a lot of ya'll but it means something to you if you're from Georgia.

We Georgians have suffered through so many years with the Falcons (the franchise began in 1966 in Atlanta), the Hawks (late sixties or early seventies I think), and the Braves (1966 as well) that I was really beginning to wonder if we would ever see a Georgia pro sports franchise win a world championship. And now, by God, I have! Watching them win it all in '95 was so exciting - you couldn't go anywhere without seeing people wearing Brave's caps and T-shirts and all the other logo stuff that was being sold by the truckloads. It was a wonderful feeling and helped us all shake the "Losersville" image that our state had for so many years.

I can remember one time during those bleak years seeing Ric Flair, the greatest wrestler that has ever lived, doing a TV interview promoting some upcoming matches. Wrestling commentator Jim Ross was interviewing him. Flair was resplendent with his long, blond hair, his expensive custom-made suit, his Rolex watch, and his gold world championship belt. Flair looked at Ross and said,

"Do you know why I make so much money, Jim Ross?"

"Why do you champ?" Ross asked.

"Cause I'm the only winning franchise that Ted Turner's got!"

exclaimed the Nature Boy.

You see, World Championship Wrestling is owned by Ted Turner. He also owns the Braves and Hawks and.........

Okay dammit, this may be hard to follow (the logic sure may be) but the Braves have been the World Champions! All you baseball lovers out there put that in your pipes and smoke it! Whooooooo!

5. Joe Tidwell committed the ultimate gaff! I never thought I would see something like this happen but I did. Joe Tidwell, a good friend of mine, did something that I will remember for a long time. And something that I have never seen anyone else do......

Joe and I worked together. Joe was a great person and friend, and we got to be very close. In fact, along with Chuck Harvey and Terry Gagnon, two more fellow employees, you could've referred to us as the Four Amigos. We were all close and saw each other at company meetings four to six times a year.

One time we had a big company confab in Arizona. We stayed at a nice resort and had several opportunities to sightsee but, of course, we were ultimately there to work. I guess a couple of days of this routine must of tired Joe out. That's the only explanation that I could come up with for what happened next.......

One evening after dinner Joe, Chuck, and I took a long walk and ended back up in Joe's room. We were all talking and Joe announced that he had to go to the bathroom. As it happened, Joe's TV had this box on it where you could order pay-per-view movies. Chuck and I examined the offerings and decided that it would be a good idea to order one. We'd have fun watching it and letting Joe pay for it made it an even better idea. So, while Joe was taking care of business in the potty, Chuck and I ordered up a soft-core porno movie. Our plan was for us to conduct a normal conversation when Joe came back in and to see how long it would take him to notice that there was less than normal programming on his television set.

Joe came out of the bathroom, plopped down on his bed, and the three of us proceeded to shoot the breeze for awhile. While we were talking, a blonde appeared on the TV screen. She was dressed in a skimpy white bathing suit and proceeded to shuck it off. Once naked, she jumped into bed with a guy that looked something like a cross between a walrus and a pink-assed ape. Anyway, Joe was talking real serious at the time, but, when this came on, he looked up and said, "What in the hell is that?" Chuck and I then told Joe that if he didn't know what it was that his marriage could be headed for serious trouble. Chuck and I laughed and 'fessed up quickly to Joe about the trick we had played on him. Joe tried to act a little indignant about it but soon he was laughing as much as Chuck or I were about the situation.

A few more minutes passed by. We were all talking and glancing at the gymnastics on the TV screen. Suddenly, in mid-sentence, Chuck looked at me and said, "Ed, check this out!"

I looked at Chuck and he pointed over to Joe. Here is Joe - Mr. Macho himself with a porno movie blaring away on his TV screen - ASLEEP on his bed! Asleep! During a porno flick!. Chuck and I compared notes and we could not think of one time during our lives that we had ever fallen asleep during a porno movie. Nor could we think of any other male that ever has.

Being the classy, decent people that Chuck and I are, we left to let Joe cut some needed Z's in his room. Of course the next morning when Chuck and I saw Joe, we ragged him mercilessly about what a man of hormones and passion he was. Joe, being the gentleman that he is, questioned our masculinity and accused us of having the sensitivity level of a desert cactus.

One thing about this experience, Joe - you never knew that it was gonna make you famous did you? I mean, everyone that reads this book will know about your exploits and you will undoubtedly be an inspiration to millions of uninspired men! Please don't thank me for giving you your "fifteen minutes of fame." The satisfaction of knowing that your exploits have been publicized is enough thanks to last a lifetime for me.

6. Willie Williams is the ugliest man in the world! Now before anything else is said, let me qualify the above by stating that Willie Williams is a dear friend of mine. A very dear friend. We met at work and became good friends almost instantly. One thing though that has characterized our relationship over the years is that we brutally rag on each other. Brutally. So here's how it goes......

Willie Williams is a good person. Loyal to his friends and will give you the shirt off his back. Not that you would want it though - cause if Willie took his clothes off, your eyes would invert and you would have to go to the hospital! For you see, Willie is ugly. Bone deep ugly! Willie is so ugly that if he ran into Freddie Krueger on the street Freddie would give him a bag to put over his head. Charlie Pound ugly (ask Ed Jr. about Charlie Pound)! Stay-in-the-house with-the-curtains-closed ugly!

One year we had a big Halloween costume contest at work. A lot of people dressed up in different costumes and some were very elaborate. While walking through the plant that morning I ran into Tony Stubbs, another good friend of mine. Tony and I were shooting the breeze when the subject of Halloween costumes came up - we were having a best costume contest that day at the plant and we gave, I think, one hundred dollars as the first prize. Tony and I started kidding that someone should dress up like Willie as he was scarier looking than most of the movie monsters people think of. Tony laughed and said, "Why don't we do it?" I personally thought it was a damn good idea and offered to help Tony put his costume together.

We got a welding jacket and cap for starters as Willie always wore these items at work. Then, we got some make-up and gave Tony's eyes a slight Oriental look as Willie somewhat favors Genghis Khan (if he was crossed with Jason Voorhees). Finally, we got together a bunch of play money as Willie is known throughout the mid-state area as a gambler and seems to always be paying off bets.

The costume contest was held at the first break period of the day. There were many elaborate costumes worn and I guess we had a good ten to fifteen people entered. When the entrants had just about all been judged the Plant Manager said that he was ready to announce the winner. I looked up and said, "Wait! There's one more entry!"

At this point, the door to the cafeteria opened and Tony came in. He crouched over like Willie does, walked into the middle of the crowd, and said, "Hey man, lemme give ya some of this jack I owe ya!"

The room convulsed in laughter - there was instant recognition as to whom Tony was impersonating!. But what was wilder than that was that Tony won, by acclamation, the one hundred dollars! Many of us laughed over this state of events until we cried....

Afterwards we all kidded Willie about being so ugly that people were using him as a model for Halloween disguises. He took this all very good naturedly and zapped me real good about a year later when we had a talent contest at work.and Willie dressed up and impersonated me. I laughed until tears came to my eyes and I think Willie did too. That was (and is) one of the best things about our friendship - we rag each other mercilessly but we both enjoy it. And if either one of us went over the line the other would say something and we would never do whatever it was again.

Willie Williams - my main man! Ugliest man in the world! And, if you ever get a chance to meet him, ask him about the time we put his name and phone number on cable channel fifteen to announce that Willie was forming a middle-Georgia Ric Flair fan club. He loves that story......

CHAPTER 8

HOLY WATER

Ed Jr. used to tell this story over the years to different people as I was growing up. I got a kick out of it then and still get a kick out of it when he tells it today. I hope anyone reading this will enjoy it half as much as I have over the years.

It seems that when my dad was growing up in the big city of Juliette that one of the big social events in the community was the yearly revival at the Juliette Methodist Church. This is the church that was used in the movie "Fried Green Tomatoes". (Remember the scene when Idgie's sister got married? Or the cemetery scene at the end of the movie when Ruth was buried? This was all filmed at the Juliette Methodist Church). Revivals at the Juliette Methodist Church were pretty tough, according to Ed Jr. They always held them in the summer when there was about one hundred and ten degree heat. My dad said that the revivals started around seven o'clock and could go for two to three hours, depending on the lung capacity of the preacher. Besides testing your stamina, you had to be still because there was nothing you would get punished for any worse than for misbehaving in church. So picture this scene in your mind - you're dressed up in your Sunday best. It's real hot, and a couple of box fans stir the hot air around. You also find yourself under attack by some pretty large mosquitoes as in Juliette they seem to get large enough to require a collar and dog tags. As you perspire profusely you are informed by the preacher in robust tones that there is a real chance that you will end up roasting in hell if you don't repent for your sins. And, you think to yourself, how could hell be much worse than sweating, swatting mosquitoes, and not being able to get up and go to the bathroom? (At a revival it was considered highly disrespectful to get up for any reason. If Mother Nature called, it had better be a major summons for you to get up and leave the service). Anyway, this was the typical nightly situation at the revivals of my dad's era.

During one particular evening of the revival Ed Jr. noticed that the preacher had brought out a container of holy water. He spent a great deal of time blessing and explaining the significance of this water. Several scriptural references were used to further illustrate the importance of the clear liquid in the fancy container. Remember now that this water was being flashed about in a room full of hot, sweaty, mosquito-swatting people.

My dad looked at the pew in front of him. In this pew sat Juanita Hardin. She was about fourteen years old at this point and probably stood six foot one. I would say she weighed about one hundred seventy-five pounds. Juanita was a large, athletic girl. She could play baseball better than most of the boys and, as a result, she was generally respected.

Ed Jr. also noted that she could beat the hell out of most of the boys and this attribute only enhanced the general feelings of respect that she generated from them.

Anyway, Juanita was sitting there. Its hot as hell and she was making no bones about it. My dad said she kept whispering about how her back was wet with sweat and how her butt itched from the pew she sat on. At this point, the preacher gets pretty dramatic and says it's now time to bless the holy water. He sets the container on a special table that is placed in front of the lectern and which sits only a few feet from the first row of pews (where Juanita happened to be sitting). After droning on about the significance of the water, he turns his back to the congregation and begins to pray. Of course, everyone in the church bowed their heads during this prayer as well.

Everyone that is, except Juanita. With an agility that most of us would envy, Juanita took two steps forward, swung her legs over the rail, grasped the container with the holy water in it, and chugged down every last drop! My dad said that the container probably held a couple of quarts of water and that Juanita drained it in about five seconds! In fact, she did this so fast that she was able to drink the water and return to her seat while the preacher was still praying.

Imagine the scene when the prayer is finished - the preacher stands up, straightens his suit, and turns to face the crowd. In facing the crowd he sees that the holy water urn is empty! Ed Jr. said that the preacher stared at the urn for the longest time and then almost fainted - he said that he could literally see his face drain of color! Apparently, the preacher interpreted this event as some sort of divine signal from the Lord. This made it even funnier to my dad as he was one of the few who looked up during the prayer and actually witnessed what Juanita did. (I asked my dad why someone didn't tell the preacher what had really happened - he said that no one would have dared do that because it would've made him look like a fool after he began preaching that the disappearance of the water was a signal from God himself). In fact, the only bad thing about this whole episode was that since the preacher thought a miracle had occurred it inspired him to preach onwards for another hour and a half. In fact, the preaching went on so long that Ed Jr. stated that some of the boys were getting pretty upset at Juanita, although, not upset enough to indicate any displeasure towards her. Finally, the service did conclude, everyone got up quickly, and hurried towards their homes.

My dad made sure that he walked home with Juanita. As they went home together, she remarked, "Hey, everybody got what they wanted! The preacher got his miracle and I got some water. What could be fairer?" My dad asked, "Aren't you afraid you'll get in trouble over this?" She replied, "Ed Williams, you're the only one that saw what happened. If I get in trouble, I'm coming to see you....."

Juanita never got one word of admonishment for what happened. And, as she got older, this story followed her til' the day she died. Even today, when my dad tells it, he'll always remark, "Ole' Nita was a good old girl."

CHAPTER 9

DR. BOLAND

It is seldom that any writer would want to do a chapter about their dentist. Typically, the associations most people make with the word "dentist" would be descriptive terms like "pain", "agony", "dealer of doom", "in-law equivalent" and others. But I cannot say this about my dentist. In fact, my dentist has made me semi-famous. In return, I will use this chapter to do the same for him.

I met Dr. Boland several years ago when Debbie and I got married. It became pretty imperative for me to find a dentist in Macon and Dr. Boland was Debbie's dentist. He takes a really personal interest in his patients and he is very easy to talk to. Over the years, we have developed a very good friendship.

Last December, I was sitting at my desk working one day and was gnawing on a stick of peppermint candy. Suddenly, there was a faint cracking sound. One of my back molars (one that I had filled as a kid with a filling the size of Plymouth Rock) had pretty much exploded. What made this sweet scenario even worse was that it occurred on December 23rd. I was sure I'd spend the next several days nursing a broken, sore tooth because Dr. Boland would be gone for the holidays.

Debbie got in touch with Dr. Boland (I hate making phone calls and avoid making them on every occasion, except of course when calling members of the Brotherhood) and phoned me. She told me that Dr. Boland was about to leave but would hold the fort until I got there. My respect for him grew even more at this display of friendship and professionalism.

I got to his office and we started kicking around politics, religion, our mutual hatred of anything that's cooked involving beets, etc.. When we got to the subject of my new tooth I said, "Doc, you ought to put a Yellow Jacket on this thing!" (For those of you who are totally out of touch with the great universities of this nation, the term Yellow Jacket is the nickname for all the athletic teams at the Georgia Institute of Technology - the academic and athletic palace of the South). Dr. Boland smiled when I mentioned the Yellow Jacket. He thought a second, looked at me and said, "Let's do it. I'll call Tech and see if I can't get a small decal. If that doesn't work, I know an artist that I believe can paint one on it." I asked, "Are you serious?" Dr. Boland replied, "Ed, you'll see when you come back in a couple of weeks." With that, he put a temporary filling in the tooth and sent me on my way.

I was so appreciative of what he'd done for me (sparing me from so much pain over the holidays) that I forgot the Yellow Jacket discussion. That is, forgot it until I returned to his office to get the permanent cap put in. I walked in and Belinda and Connie, two of his very capable assistants, greeted me. I noticed in their greetings a little levity and a certain sparkle in their eyes. I either had to believe that the Yellow Jacket tooth was a reality or that Belinda and Connie had simultaneously fallen in love with me. Since I knew the odds on the latter, I figured Dr. Boland had scored the tooth.

A few minutes went by and I was escorted into one of Dr. Boland's patient areas. After awhile the Doc came in and was smiling like a mule that's eaten a mouthful of briars. Hiding one arm behind his back, he slowly moved it into view to reveal a cap with a perfect Yellow Jacket design on it! I was so impressed - it was a very detailed miniature decal. As I expressed my delight, the Doc informed me that it was not a decal but a painting! He had had an artist friend of his paint a Yellow Jacket on the tooth. Then, Dr. Boland proceeded to join the immortals of my lifetime by informing me that this priceless artwork was on the house. I expressed even more gratitude and told the Doc to put the cap in my mouth before he changed his mind or something.

I'd be lying if I told you how much I enjoyed Dr. Boland putting that cap in - I'd rather have eaten a fire ant mound than to have endured the procedure. But, once in, I had a piece of artwork in my mouth that would last forever. The best thing about it all is that no one can see the design unless I show it to them (I have to pull my lip back for it to be visible). It's like having a tattoo, only it can be displayed whenever I want to show it.

I went home in a real good mood until I got about two hundred yards from the house. At this point it hit me that I would have to show Debbie the tooth!. Since Debbie is pretty straight-laced, I got concerned very quickly that she might not take to the artwork very well. But, well or not, Buzz (the official name of the beloved Yellow Jacket mascot) was on my tooth to stay as he is sealed on there with a clear acrylic coating. I walked into the house not quite knowing what to expect.

Upon entering, Debbie said hello and asked me the usual questions about my day. I mumbled the answers hoping that she had forgotten about the cap. Of course, she immediately asked me about it and how it felt. I told her that there were no problems and that I was feeling okay. She then asked me to see the cap. I reluctantly pulled my lip back. Debbie leaned forward, peered closely into my mouth, and exclaimed, "Edward, my God!" I always know that I'm in trouble whenever Debbie changes my name from Ed to Edward. I calmly explained to her what had happened and how proud she should be of Dr. Boland's efforts. She was not terribly happy with the explanation until I showed her that Buzz could not be seen unless my lip was pulled back. Once she was assured of that she seemed a little more content and started talking about something else.

A few minutes later Alison and Will came strolling into the kitchen. They asked me if they could see my tooth as they had heard some stray bits of the conversation Debbie and I had just finished. Alison, of course, walks up first and asks, "Let me see the tooth, Dad." I showed it to her. Her only remark was, "Cool." Will had an even better response. After looking at it, Will immediately walked over to Debbie and asked if he could have something painted on one of his teeth.

A couple of months later I was eating dinner and noticed, yet again, that one of my lower molars had broken away. I called Dr. Boland and made yet another trek to his office. I got there, sat down in the chair, and the Doc tells me that I need another cap. In discussing this, he asks if I want some artwork on it? Since this tooth is visible when I smile or talk, I tell him that I don't want anything. Of course, for anyone reading this, it just shows how truly henpecked I am.

What I didn't realize was that Dr. Boland was about to set a new standard as regards being henpecked! On the day that I came in to get the cap, he informed me that he almost put an elephant on the tooth. The elephant was the Doc's way of acknowledging my Republican leanings. I thought that this was a great idea but when Dr. Boland wheeled the tooth out, alas, it had no elephant! I was fairly disappointed and then Dr. Boland tells me that he was worried that Debbie would get upset with him if he decorated another tooth. I told him, "Damn Doc, it's bad enough for me to be henpecked but Deb's got you too!" I guess Debbie's ability to henpeck extends beyond me and into my immediate circle of friends. I don't really know what else once could say about this, but you can't help but be a little bit impressed by it.

Well that's all I got to say, Doc. Maybe this'll bring in a few more customers. Remember one thing though - don't accept any requests for bulldog logo teeth.

CHAPTER 10

RON MILLER,
JOCKITCH PROFESSOR

Ron Miller is a real good friend of mine. We worked together for a couple of years - I as a Plant Human Resources Manager, Ron as the Safety and Environmental Manager. Ron is a very kind-hearted person and is also one of the most intense individuals that I have ever met. He is one of those guys that plays checkers like the fate of the world hinges upon the outcome. We always referred to Ron as a pit bulldog - he has a tenacity that serves him well in many ways. He is also one of the kindest and most thoughtful people you will ever meet. And, as you are about to find out, he was the subject of one of the best practical jokes I have ever had the fun of sharing.

Ron was just getting started in his new job. He was organizing our safety committees and trying to make some sense out of our workmen's comp administration. He was making good progress but, as most intense individuals are wont to do, was frustrated at the speed of progress he was making. These qualities caused him to be accepted very quickly at our plant but also contributed to how badly he fell for what I'm about to tell you.

One day Mark Salter, who at that time was a Shift Supervisor, walked into my office to shoot the breeze. This was around May or June of 1994 and it was hot as hell in the plant. Mark came in sweating profusely and elaborated at length as to how hot it was and how tired he was. Mark went on to mention that the heat and humidity was such that he is going to have a world class case of jock itch. We laughed about this and then Mark said, "I ought to go up and see Ron and ask him if jock itch is covered under workmen's compensation!"

It didn't take long for the wheels to begin turning. The first thought that hit me was how totally absurd it would be to file a claim for jock itch under workmen's comp. Then I began thinking about how seriously Ron would take a scenario like this. More thoughts came to me as to how Cecil Asbell, our no-nonsense Production Manager, would feel about a comp claim like that. He would not only be disgusted but would also feel like Ron was not really doing his job. As I kept thinking this whole scenario's possibilities began to grow.....

It took Mark and I a couple of minutes to devise the plot for this scam. Now, before we go further, you should know that Mark is six foot five and weighs about two hundred sixty pounds. He's a big man and has even wrestled professionally in the past. The reason I tell you this is because, if you've ever watched pro wrestling (really the only sport you can depend on for any level of consistency any more), you know that these guys have to be good actors. The interviews and hypes for the next pay-per-view matches are what sells wrestling. This explains how Mark, after leaving my office, was able to go upstairs and give Ron a very believable spiel on how he was suffering from plutonium strength jock-itch. He told Ron in great detail as to when he first noticed the itch, how it burned, and how the chafe was so bad that he wanted to go to the doctor. Mark ended his remarks by asking Ron if workmen's comp was gonna pick up the bill?

Ron very nearly had four strokes trying to explain to Mark that jock itch would not be covered under workmen's compensation! Mark, in a very professional way, explained to Ron that he had gotten it while working and went on to expound on how Ron's attitude regarding his problem was unprofessional. You could've poached an egg on Ron's forehead (actually, it's a fivehead as Ron has about as much hair on his head as a bass) as Mark made that statement. Then, Ron asked Mark questions about recent sports activities he had participated in that could've caused the jock itch. Finally he barraged Mark with other questions regarding Mark's jock itch history. Mark said afterwards that Ron knew more about his groin and its fungal infection history than any person on the face of the earth. "I guess it's something to be proud off", I said to Mark as we both convulsed in laughter over these shenanigans.

It didn't take long until Ron was in my office. He had his bulldog face going and his first words were, "We have a little problem here chief." He then goes on to explain how Mark claims he picked up jock itch on the job, etc, etc. Ron is very sincere as he explains this - I was just glad that Mark had been in my office a few minutes earlier and that we had already laughed hard over this scam. I looked Ron directly in the eye and asked him how he could let this happen? Ron said, "Chief, I'll do everything within my power to see that this claim doesn't get paid!" I told Ron, "You'd better! We didn't hire a Safety Manager to come in here and give away workmen's comp funds on jock itch cases!" Ron assured me that everything would be taken care of - I told him I had confidence in him and let him go on about his business.

We let a couple of days go by and then Mark left Ron a voice mail message. It seemed, he told Ron, that "the itch is getting worse and I need you to make me an appointment with the doctor. I can't even stand up or sit down without pain and I need you to help me! Ron, so help me, I got this damn rot on the job!" Mark exclaims and then hangs up.

Ron comes down to see me again. He was trying to hedge his bets. "I'm working like hell on this chief, but, I'm not sure whether or not this qualifies as workmen's comp. But I can tell you this - we're fighting it every step of the way!" I told Ron that that wasn't good enough. "Ron", I said "You need to have a heart-to-heart with Mark. He'll realize how this situation looks and will work with us. But, you've got to talk with him soon! And, most importantly of all, whatever you do don't let him go to one of our comp doctors! If he does that, we're dead." Ron assures me that everything will be taken care of and he left the office.

As soon as Ron was gone, I primed one of our HR Clerks about this situation. She was more than glad to help participate in our scheme. After a couple of days she calls Ron and tells him that she's gotten a bill from one of our comp doctors for Mark Salter's jock itch. She asked Ron if she should proceed to process the claim? Ron comes down to my office again to see me.

"Chief, I hate to tell you this, but Salter went to a comp doctor with jock itch." Ron grudgingly spat out. "I know Dr. Splinflatz and I'll talk this over with him. We'll cut this off before it goes any further." I replied, "You damn well better cut this off! Now, that it's gone to a comp doctor Cecil will have to know. Ron, what do you think Cecil will say when I tell him that we have a new Safety Manager who's telling us that we're going to have to pay for a claim for jock itch?" Ron looked really serious and said that he was going to call some friends of his over the weekend that could give him good professional advice regarding this situation. I told him that if it would help to call Marcus Welby, MD. Ron left my office yet again and we all went home for the weekend.

By now, we've run this gag for over a week. A lot of people got in on it, but to their credit no one said anything to Ron. Monday morning came and Ron walked into my office and said, "Chief, I'm concerned. I talked with my old boss over the weekend and he said that this jock itch situation with Mark Salter is serious. He feels that it would qualify for payment under the workmen's comp laws. I don't like telling you this but I made five phone calls over the weekend and talked to everyone whom I felt had some knowledge on this subject. All of them said that this case is potential workmen's comp. I have to tell you the truth."

All of ya'll reading this would've been extremely proud of me at this point. I was very empathetic towards Ron and his plight. I told him not to worry and that we'd do whatever we had to do to correct this situation. I then remarked that I appreciated Ron's efforts and that his perseverance was admirable. All in all, I must've given him a good five to ten minutes of this drivel. Ron listened to it, believed it, and thanked me for being so understanding. I told him that I was proud of him and would totally support him if this thing did become a comp case. Ron walked out in a few minutes looking much more relieved than when he first came in.

As soon as I was sure Ron was gone I called Cecil on the phone. I asked him to come by my office as I needed to discuss something important with him. He appeared a few minutes later.

Cecil strolled into my office and I informed him about the latest developments with Ron regarding the jock itch situation. I mentioned to Cecil that Ron was trying to prepare us for the fact that this jock itch scenario might very well be classified as a workmen's comp case. "Could it really be one?" Cecil asked. I told Cecil that it could be but that we had more important things to do than discuss the workmen's comp merits of jock itch. Cecil laughed and agreed. Then he said, "Well, now that Ron's feeling better about this jock itch stuff, I guess that I'll need to go up and tell him that there's no way in hell that this can become a comp claim!" I told Cecil that this was a direct contradiction to what Ron and I had just talked about. Cecil smiled and said, "I know", and walked out.

You couldn't have paid me enough money not to eavesdrop on the conversation Cecil had with Ron. As soon as Cecil left my office he went upstairs to see Ron in the penthouse (we referred to Ron's office as the penthouse because it was directly over mine and was once the trucker's lounge). Cecil walked in and Ron was on the phone....

"Get off that damn phone!" Cecil shouts.

Ron puts down the phone and says, "What's up, big man?"

Cecil replies, "I'll tell you what's up. I want to know if you're serious about paying workmen's comp for this jock itch thing?"

Ron states, "It's not what I want to do CL (Cecil's first two initials) but it may be what we have to do."

"Why in the hell do we have to do that?"

"Well, Mark can make a pretty convincing case that he got jock itch doing his job. If he can establish that, he'll get the comp."

Cecil's face got red. He said, "Ron, is this why we hired you? We get a new Safety Manager and pay you all this damn money so that you can pay off claims for jock itch? What in the hell are you good for? You're supposed to help me, not hurt me! Dammit, what is corporate gonna say about all this?" Cecil goes on to give Ron about five minutes more of this type grief. At the end of the tirade, Ron says that he will do anything to help Cecil and that he's sure he can keep this from being a comp case.

Cecil walked out of Ron's office and down to mine. We laughed so hard that my rib cage hurt the next day. Cecil and I both agreed that Ron had passed his rituals of manhood test with flying colors. We also both agreed that Cecil had missed his true calling as he should be out in Hollywood based on the acting abilities he had just displayed. Cecil laughed and said, "I was pretty good, wasn't I?" I laughed again and agreed that he was. Then Cecil, in a true humanitarian gesture, said that he felt that we had kept the heat on Ron long enough and that we should tell him that this whole thing was a practical joke. I had to agree with him. We called Ron and asked him to come down to my office.

Ron came in and sat down. Cecil and I slowly laid out the details of the joke we had played on him. Ron had the strangest look on his face that I have ever seen in my life. I expected Ron to be angry, embarrassed, or something, but the look I saw on his face expressed relief!

"Damn right I'm relieved!" Ron exclaimed. "Think about how you'd feel if you had gone to college four years, studied like hell, got a degree in a safety/environmental discipline, and then find out that it was all gonna be blown down the toilet over a case of jock itch!"

We all laughed, and then the three of us replayed the joke again and laughed over and over and over. Cecil and I afterwards, in separate conversations with Ron, laid all the responsibility for the joke on the other (just to let you know how strong our characters are). Besides the laughs, Ron actually earned a lot of respect over how he handled this situation. He was determined, did his research, and did everything he knew to straighten the problem out. You couldn't have asked for more. That's one of the reasons Ron will be remembered at the plant and will be a good friend of mine for as long as we both live. He's that kind of guy. Just don't let him buy concessions for you at a ball game and you'll be okay.

CHAPTER 11

BANKING

This will not be a long chapter as I will not discuss this field of endeavor any longer than I have to. However, there are some very interesting things concerning the banking business that I would like to relate here........

1. It's a very boring field. Ever notice the type people that work in banks? Most of them wouldn't know excitement if you poked them with a cattle prod. They may be very nice people but they're also dull. Very dull. Since banks offer investment opportunities that are for the most part conservative, they have to recruit and hire dull people.

2. It's the biggest ass-kissing field of endeavor on this planet. We have tons of banks here in Macon so it must be both a profitable and somewhat cutthroat business. Because of these qualities bank employees must royally kiss each customer's ass. You don't believe this? Well, I've done my research folks. Went to a local branch bank the other day and positioned myself at a counter and acted like I was filling out some papers. From where I stood I could hear the conversations the tellers were having. They went something like this:

"Mr. Smith, it's such a pleasure to see you (to a guy known around Macon as a fourteen karat horse's ass). You light up this bank when you come in!"

"It's only for preferred customers such as yourself that we offer these type credit card rates!" (This to a person that couldn't get credit at a convenience store, much less anywhere else).

"I'm sure your wife Nora will love the new diamond ring you bought her. Let's talk about that line of credit you need." (This guy is a known philanderer and was even flirting with the teller).

Such bullshit has to be perversely admired. It is this quality that leads many from the banking field into the political arena. In fact, come to think of it, banking is the ideal training ground for politics. The traits needed for both professions are incredibly similar.

3. Banks give out the biggest titles in the world but pay the people holding them nothing. Ever notice that anyone that works in a bank has a title like "Vice President of Lending Services", or "Director of Branch Operations", or "Assistant Vice President of Car Loan Financing?" In fact, what in the hell is an Assistant Vice President? If anyone knows, I'd sure like to because I don't understand the position at all. Even with all these big titles the people in the jobs make little money. Several years ago I got a resume that was sent in from someone in the banking field. The resume was a lengthy recitation of banking accomplishments. This person held the position of "Assistant Vice President of Something." Sounds really lofty, huh? You wanna know what their current salary was - $18,000! No wonder they wanted to seek another job opportunity! (One word to the wise for those of you out there that decide the names of these banking positions - change the position titles. You don't know how many laughs I have exchanged over the years with other human resources managers over the VP-No Bucks titles). An assistant manager at a McDonald's makes more money than that! And, worse yet, because these people have a title, they get drastically overblown opinions of their self-worth. I interviewed one of these types a few years back and was amazed at how picky they were about the jobs they would take and how unrealistic their salary expectations were. It's amazing how a title and a suit can totally blow some people's perspectives. This leads me to......

4. Bank employees have to dress up all the time for work. I will credit them with this - they look good. I guess if you had to live on $18,000 a year that looking good compensates for the low income.

Personally, I'd rather shovel shit and make some money but that's a different subject for a different time. The one thing that you have to wonder about though is how do they buy all these nice clothes while making so little money? Undoubtedly, there must be a special loan department in the bank that gives their employees loans for the clothes that they must have. Maybe they get a tax deduction for having to buy these clothes? Who knows? Better yet, who cares?

I can remember when I went to grad school a few years back that a lot of the people in my classes were from local area banks. Apparently, banks love for you to have good educational credentials beside your name. Not that you'll get paid for them of course, but they do look good. These guys and ladies would constantly use four dollar words about amortization schedules, credit card nuances, and the like. They smiled all the time and, if you tried talking with them, they spoke somewhat condescendingly to you (or anyone else outside of their clique). It was like they were snubbing people, but, given the facts, just exactly who they were snubbing was a mystery to me. Several of us in the class could have bought and sold most of them several times over but they continued being elitist. It was almost amusing.

Maybe that quality summarizes my disdain for the banking business. It is involved far too much in appearances and not enough in realities. I appreciate realness and even earthiness much more than I do plasticness (this is a new word I invented) and phoniness. This concludes my diatribe about banking except for one more thing.....

Next time you have some people over to your house that you want to get rid of, tell them you're having to make an emergency run to the bank and invite them to go with you. If that doesn't cause them to leave and go home, nothing will.

CHAPTER 12

PORNO MOVIES

Before anyone gets upset and thinks that this is going to be a "nasty" chapter, don't worry - it won't be. There are just some interesting things that I've picked up from porno movies over the years that I wanted to talk with you about. It isn't that I've watched that many of them, but any man that tells you that they haven't watched one of these things is telling a bald-faced lie. That's all. I promise to be brief, elegant, and tasteful in the discussion. You believe that? Good. Let's talk.....

The first thing that's very apparent if you watch one of these things is that there is an inverse relationship between breast/genitalia size and one's acting ability. The people that cast these movies must find their thespians on street corners, note the size of their "assets" and say, "You're destined to be a porno movie actor." I'll bet that no porno movie actor/actress ever quit over script content or artistic disagreements with the director. In fact, most of the scripts seem to be created as the movie is being filmed. This creativity in and of itself is interesting and deserves some discussion.

Ever noticed the positions used by porno actors and actresses during the multiple sex acts in these films? I've watched a few of these movies and have seen it done.....

...on the floor....

...up against a refrigerator...

...with the woman leaning over a trashcan in a vacant alley...

...with the woman straddling a staircase...

...with the man sitting on a motorcycle...

...with the woman lying on a pool table...

...in a steam room....

And in a zillion and one other places and positions. I'm convinced that these movies cause injuries every year because you can't tell me that there aren't couples out there that don't try some of the featured positions. They get started and find out that to be successful your genitalia size must be godzillian. If you're not suitably endowed, you're bound to hurt yourself.

I've always wondered how a person performs the sex act in front of several cameras, directors, props people, and anyone else that's happens to be around while the scene is being filmed. I don't think I could be paid enough money to do that. (Besides, I wouldn't even pay to watch myself having sex, much less expect others to pay for it). I mean, don't you know there's a lot of snickering and face making directed at the "actors"/"actresses"? I would be hollering stuff like, "Nice pimple on the ass there," or, "Gee, you can barely see the implant scars", or other such niceties. They must either pay these people a lot of money or they are true exhibitionists and would do this for little or no money at all. Well, if you're gonna do it indiscriminately you may as well get paid for it. We all ultimately pay for sex, one way or the other.

You don't believe that? Consider this for a second - what really motivates us to work hard, save money, and improve our lifestyles? If you don't say sex you're kidding yourself. Beyond food and shelter, what else is there? You can say all you want to about stimulating your mind and I'll bet that a whole lot of you read to stimulate your minds, right? That's why you're reading this - you're reading it to get a laugh, or maybe even one or two insights that might help you. Makes you feel good about yourself, hmm? If you get right down to it though I'll bet that most of the readers of this book, given the choice, would much rather be having sex than reading this. That's the whole point isn't it? Find me someone who would prefer reading over sex and I'll show you someone with an incurable disease or someone that needs to have their IQ tested. Sex is the driver for a lot of the things that we do. And we all ultimately pay for sex.

Debbie and I got into a little debate a while back over the "we all pay for sex" issue. It seems that one evening after I got home from work Debbie began talking to me about something she had seen on one of those TV talk shows. Apparently Donahue or Jenny Jones or whomever was hosting the show had four prostitutes on as guests. These ladies described how they made their living, how much money the pimp got, why they were doing it, etc. Debbie explained the gist of the show to me and then expressed horror that these women could perform sexual acts for money.

I thought for a second and the whole conversation sort of triggered something in my mind. I looked over at Debbie and asked her, "How often do I get paid?"

"Once every two weeks," she replied.

"And what do I do with the check?" I asked.

Debbie replied, "You give it all to me and my God Edward! How you can equate that to prostitution is beyond me!!"

I gave her my most serious, pensive, Foskey-type look and said, "I really can't equate it to prostitutes babe. After all, if I went to a prostitute I'd have some money left over afterwards!"

Debbie started to really get upset but then she realized I was kidding her. There is a little truth in what I told her though. For all you guys out there it's okay to think this kind of stuff, but, don't be a dummy like me and openly express your thoughts to your wife on this. Mine is used to me being off the wall but I don't want to get letters from any of ya'll telling me that you made a comment like this and got thrown out of the house, or a letter from a divorce attorney, or worse. It's okay to think it - just don't say it. This profound thought is a valuable guide for success in any marriage.

Let's get back to the porno movie stuff. Undoubtedly most of the buyers or renters of skin flicks are men. In fact, it seems like I saw some study somewhere that indicated that seventy to eighty percent of porno movie patrons are men. I don't understand why we guys get such a kick out of watching porno flicks but we do. Actually, our wives should love that we watch them. Ever sat down and watched one of these movies? If you don't feel like taking the wife upstairs and doing the horizontal mambo afterwards then something is wrong with you. (In fact, the best "I want to have sex" movie I ever saw was one of these R-rated jobs called "Private Lessons." It had that gal in it that played Emmanuelle, Sylvia Crystal. If she doesn't make you want to have sex, get a glass of Bosco and watch Captain Kangeroo or something as you are beyond hope (or at least beyond hormones).

Technology has made porno movies much more popular now. Used to be, if you wanted to see an X-rated flick you had to go to an adult theater. Now this was a risky proposition at best. First, you didn't dare want someone that knew you to see you going into one of these theaters. Friends of mine who went to them invariably reported running into their preachers as they snuck in, or in-laws, or whatever. Secondly, you have to sit there and act like you're watching the movie for its artistic merits. Lastly, due to some of the acts of the more disgusting patrons of the theater, you never knew what you might be sitting in.

The advent of mass-produced VCRs in the early eighties changed all this. With VCRs you could rent videos and watch these movies in the privacy of your home. I well remember the first time I saw a porno video on a VCR. It occurred back in 1984 when I worked at NYK. Bernie Simmons, at that time the VP of Manufacturing, purchased a VCR for his home. It also happened that Jimmy Joyner, the facility HR Manager and my boss at the time, had his house all to himself for a few nights as his family was away visiting relatives. After finding out that one member of our group had a porn video, a plan was devised whereby we would have Bernie bring his VCR over to Jimmy's house. Once there, about six or seven of us would watch this video. We were all fired up about testing this new technology.

About eight of us strolled into Jimmy's house that evening. We were all laughing and smiling and having a good 'ol time. It couldn't help but bring to mind the old proverb about men being little boys at heart. We were all acting like kids that were doing something forbidden and were enjoying it to the max. Bernie came in a little late and proceeded to hook his VCR up to the TV. Jimmy was nice enough to have purchased us a few beers and popcorn and other assorted movie junk. (The only thing about this though is it raises the question as to who wants to eat junk food while watching someone's heinie bounce up and down on the screen? One thing I have noticed in these movies is that not every actor or actress in them is going to win beauty awards - which in and of itself doesn't stimulate the desire to eat).

The movie started and we all were immediately transfixed. John Holmes was the star of this particular epic, which was aptly titled "Come Again." Big John played a mailman that made a whole lot of personal stops on his rounds. For those of you unfamiliar with John Holmes let's just say that he is the poster boy for the term "well-endowed." Big John measured about fourteen inches, which definitely contributed towards his successful career in the adult movie business (I saw an article in a magazine one time where John said he'd had sex with about twenty thousand women over the span of his illustrious career. I'm sure these women feel good now about their encounters after it came out that Big John died of AIDS a few years ago). As we sat there, the movie started and the plot began to unfold. Apparently, in the neighborhood where Big John delivered the mail, all the women had the morals of Brazilian wharf rats. It seemed that every home Big John came to revealed that the woman was home, alone, and had pants hotter than Three Mile Island. In scene after scene Big John did his thing with a variety of willing young women.

I was panning my eyes around the room to gauge the reactions to this flick. Everyone seemed to be pretty focused on the movie, especially Mr. Hitami, who was one of our Japanese engineers. You could say stuff to him as the movie was going on and he would not respond as he was so transfixed with the on-screen shenanigans. When Big John took on two neighborhood beauties at the same time, I thought Mr. Hitami was going to burst out cheering or something.

A slight problem developed as we watched the movie. While it was running I drank two or three cokes and mother nature began signaling me that I needed to visit the head. The only problem with doing this was that we all had been kidding each other about who was going to have to go to the bathroom to "relieve" themselves first. I had been doing a lot of the kidding, so, I guess it was only right that I had to go first. I held it as long as I could - then, when the pressure got too immense, I bravely stood up and said, "I gotta go take a leak."

The guys in the room busted out laughing. There were crude

remarks made about "choking the pony" and other similar type statements. I told the group they were all sick but, no matter what, I hadda go pee! The laughter got worse as I flipped them off and went into the bathroom.

I walked into the bathroom (which was right off the den where we were watching the movie). It hit me when I strolled in that if I left the door open these guys could hear me peeing and no remarks about me flogging the puppy would filter back to the plant. So that's what I did. And I made sure that those guys knew it. Picture it - a grown man, twenty-eight at the time, standing in a bathroom with his dick in his hands, announcing to a group that he is peeing. These guys actually quieted down some after I made my announcement. I also noticed when I got back that several of them then made the trip to the bathroom. Sometimes, you know, it takes one brave pioneer to blaze the trail for the others.......

Did you ever notice how guys in these porno flicks always pull out at the moment of truth and blast all over the girl? It would be bad enough to be buck nekkid in front of a room full of people but to have to do that too? I don't think so - I would rather read the Koran or something as opposed to having to do perform that duty. But, I guess it reinforces the fact that most of us do have a price - some's prices are higher than others - and will do almost anything for the long green (which would be a good title for a porno flick starring the Jolly Green Giant).

One thing to remember as I mercifully bring this chapter to a close - you may have laughed or been offended by my writings but, one thing's for sure - you had a reaction. What does this tell me? Well, if you had a reaction, it can only mean that you've watched porno movies before. Go ahead and admit it. We all have watched them at one time or the other. It sort of reminds me of a discussion we had one time in my Sunday School class. Everyone in there talks against the lottery, but, at one point during a discussion about the lotto, several of my classmates explained and understood perfectly how the games worked. Admit it - we all indulge in a little sinful activity every now and then. I actually think its healthy - you can't fight the war against sin unless you understand exactly what it is. And most times I seem to understand it pretty clearly.

CHAPTER 13

VASECTOMY

Let's be really clear before we get this chapter started. One, I agree that the permanent birth control procedure for men is much simpler than the procedure for women is. All the medical journals and experts state this as well, so who am I to disagree? Two, I also agree that if a woman can deliver children that the man should then do his part when the time for permanent birth control arrives. (If you can't understand the need for permanent birth control, read chapter eight, item fifteen. This is the material concerning buying prophylactics at X-Mart. If that doesn't inspire you to undertake permanent birth control, nothing will). I totally agree with all of the above things. So much so that yours truly has had, performed on him, the dreaded "V". I've had it done and am proud to say I've had it done. But let me get one thing on the record.....

It hurts like HELL! I can think of no injury or pain I've ever suffered that was worse! It was so bad that even Debbie felt sorry for me. But, before we go any further, let's start at square one and track through how my "V" came about in the first place. Once I set the stage, I'll take all you guys out there through every excruciating detail about the procedure. I want you to be knowledgeably armed so that if you get pushed into doing this (but don't want it done) you can use this book as your main point of defense! Men, sit down in a secure chair, cross your legs and squeeze them tightly, and read about the horrors

I endured in the name of family planning.

To begin with, Debbie and I felt that two children was the right number for us to have. This was regardless of what sex they turned out to be. As it worked out, we had a girl and a boy, which was great. However, in the fall of 1988, we began serious discussions regarding the "V". Debbie's arguments were logical - it's easier for the male, I've had two children, you can do this, etc. They all made sense and I readily agreed to do my thing for the good of the family.

The first thing I needed to know, because of my ignorance, was just who does these vasectomies? I figured general practitioners must handle them but I was quickly corrected and told that urologists perform these procedures. I had no problem with that - after all, a doctor that spends extensive time handling problems associated with men's penises should be able to handle vasectomies. With that question answered, I figured Debbie would work out the details and I would show up one day, get clipped, and go home. I found out that there is a helluva lot more to it than that.

Debbie informed me that in a couple of weeks we had an appointment with Dr. Fletcher, noted Macon urologist. "We?" I asked. I was under the mistaken conclusion that all the work was being done on my privates. Debbie confirmed that it was my privates that were getting worked on but that the first step was for both of us to see the doctor. This was being done so that he could walk us through the procedure and answer any questions that we might have. Well, I told Debbie that I understood the procedure and that this was not necessary but Debbie still felt we needed to visit him. This was one of the biggest mistakes I ever made in my life, as you will soon see.

If I remember right, the appointment was made for about three o'clock in the afternoon on a Thursday. (I'll bet you're surprised that someone that can hardly remember what they did last weekend would remember this much detail. I assure you, ask any veteran that was on Normandy Beach if they remember it. They do - and this was about as traumatic for me as Normandy Beach was for them). We walked in, sat down and waited for, I guess, about thirty minutes. The nurse asked me when I checked in what I was there for? I replied that I was getting a vasectomy. She gave me a knowing smile, had me sign a couple of papers, and told me to wait.

This same nurse told us about forty-five minutes later that Dr. Fletcher was ready to see us. I bounded into the room and Debbie and I shook hands with the doc and all the appropriate introductions were made. We all sat down in some comfortable easy chairs and then our discussion began.

The first thing I noticed, even before we got started good, was that Dr. Fletcher had received his medical degree from the University of Georgia School of Medicine! I was very shook up. I couldn't believe that I, a loyal Georgia Tech fan, a bleeder of yellow and navy blue, a wearer of the Tech logo on one of my teeth, was going to put my most prized possession on the chopping block for a UGA doctor! It defied belief! At this point, I could take the queasy feeling that I already had, multiply it by three, and it might describe to you how I was feeling. A University of Georgia doctor? Given my profound respect for the school, I might as well have gotten a Zambesi root doctor to alter my poor member. At this point there was one thing for certain - I was damn well not going to mention my love of Georgia Tech to this doctor. If I did that, he would probably remove my privates and dangle them from his car mirror like those fuzzy dice that you see sometimes.

The doctor began the session by explaining the procedure. Apparently, there are a couple of tubes going into my you-know-what that carry the sperm cells. A vasectomy effectively cuts these two tubes so that sperm never gets to where it needs to go. This keeps you from visiting the prophylactics display at X-Mart for the rest of your life. The doctor pointed to a chart on the wall that showed all the plumbing inside the male genitalia and what was going to happen to mine.

I really started getting squeamish - it was one thing to do this, but, to have to see how its actually done really started to make me feel ill. So much so that I remember crossing my legs in a vise-like grip that would have taken the threat of death itself to get me to release. The more I heard the about this procedure, the more scared I got. So much so that I started thinking this weird, stereotypical stuff that all guys think when they have a vasectomy. Stuff like:

"After it's done, will I just want to lay around and eat?"

"Will I not have a temper anymore and just be docile?"
"Will I begin to get extremely interested in art?"
"Will I be able to enjoy sex as I have known it in the past?"
"Will I want to learn to crochet?"

The doc continued to drone on. After a while he asked us if we met his criteria for a vasectomy. "What criteria is that?" I asked. The doc said that because of the permanence of the surgery (the good doc not only severed the tubes but cauterized the ends of them as well. Are you getting a little more squeamish now, guys? Believe you me, this is only the tip of the iceberg as you will soon find out) that couples had to meet certain criteria he had established before he would perform it. He then explained that to perform the surgery the male had to be at least thirty years of age, the couple had to have had at least two children, and that both are absolutely convinced that this is the route they want to take. I assured the doc that I met all the criteria - I was thirty-two years old in 1988, I had Alison and Will, and I was (and still am) convinced that two children were all I wanted. He said okay and started to talk with us about scheduling the surgery.

"How long does it take, Doc?" I inquired.
"About twenty to twenty-five minutes, Ed." he replied.
"Are you going to put me under sedation?"
"Just a local anesthetic, Ed." said Doc.
."Ummmmmm - just how is that anesthetic administered?" I asked.
"By needle, Ed." Doc replied.
"And where does that needle go, Doc?" I gulped.
"We insert it into the scrotum, Ed." Doc quickly responded.

Now guys - don't you feel just wonderful knowing this? Personally, I hate getting a shot in the arm. Guess what I felt like knowing that the needle was going to go into my scrotum? It was too horrible to even think about!
"Doc, isn't there some alternative method for the anesthesia?" I stammered.
"Ed, if I put you under full sedation, you'd have to spend the night at the hospital. This surgery is now only considered a same day

outpatient type procedure. If I did what you wanted, your insurance wouldn't cover it and you'd have to pay extra."

"I'm willing to pay extra, Doc. There're only my genitals," I replied.

"Ed, trust me, you won't even know you're having the surgery," said Doc. A bigger lie has never been told.

The doc rattled off a few more things about my impending doom. For some strange reason, I started to feel more relaxed. Looking back on this, I'm sure that this was a self-defense mechanism triggered by my brain. I mean, think about it - what was there to be relaxed about? I'm about to get my genitalia cut, I'm thinking and believing I'm gonna lose my manhood, and I had another embarrassing concern that one of my buddies at work brought up. It went something like, "What happens if you go in there and drop your pants and a cute nurse is there and you get erect? What would you do?"

I immediately told this guy that he was a sick son-of-a-bitch. But it did make me wonder - what would I do? Added to the other list of concerns, I could see that this was a fine damn situation that I was finding myself locked into.

While all these thoughts swirled around in my head, the doc continued to drone on. Something about us being sure about having the procedure done. I damn well wasn't sure but at this point it's sort of like when you go with a group to an amusement park. Those big roller coasters can really look intimidating but you get on them because of the group. You don't want to be the wimp, the party pooper, the weenie, or whatever. It was the same here with the vasectomy - I didn't dare tell the doc or Debbie that I wanted to wimp out. I had to go through with it.

Once I came to that conclusion, I lightened up. I was gonna do it so why not ask some questions and really get involved in the experience? I cleared my throat and asked the doc, "Tell me again about cutting the tubes. Where are they - are they close to the surface or do you have to go in deep?"

The doc gave me a serious look, stood up, and said, "Ed, follow me." We walked into a little room just off his office. I quickly glanced around and noticed an examination table, a sink, and other types of medical paraphernalia. Before I had a real chance to drink it all in, the doc says, "Ed, pull down your pants and get up here on the table."

I was somewhat surprised so I asked, "Why, Doc?" The doc replied, "I'm going to show you exactly where the tubes are that get severed (this thought alone was enough for me to instinctively clamp my legs together)."

I unpry my legs, drop my pants, and get up on the table. Doc puts his hand on my do-lolly to hold it up and then with his other hand pinches the shit out of my scrotum. He does this to show me where the tubes are that would be cut. At this point, I have quickly learned two things:

1. It hurts like hell to have someone pinch your scrotum. I don't care who does it. If your wife or girlfriend or mistress or whatever says they want to do this to you, don't let them. The pain is fierce - the scrotum is meant to dangle and swing, not be pinched.

2. The next thing that hit me was that a man was handling my dingus. I couldn't stand this. I have many faults, and to each his own, but I am not a homosexual. I never have been nor will I ever be. Even thinking about sex with a man is enough to make me gag. Now, I'm lying on this table, and after thirty-two years of life I have a fifty-plus year old man handling my dick. It was the most squeamish, ill feeling that I think I've ever had in my life. The only thing that I could think of was that this man made a living by handling men's dicks. And, it was a legitimate occupation and he had a license to practice it. Only in America......

The doc finally took his hand off my weenie and let me up off the table. I couldn't get up fast enough. He looked at me and said, "Ed, now do you understand the procedure you will undergo?" I told the doc that I did. Hell, what else could I say? If I told him I still didn't understand the procedure it might mean that I'd have to drop my drawers and let the him examine me again. I damn well wasn't gonna do that. I thanked the doc for his time and effort and we walked back into his main office.

We all talked a little while longer and the doc tells us that we appear to be ready for this procedure. Debbie might be ready, and the doc might be, but I sure as hell wasn't. But, at this point, my proverbial goose was cooked. I was gonna have to have this done and get it over with. We both got up, thanked the doc for his time, and Deb and I went home.

On our way home Debbie talked to me but I listened to very little of what she was saying. I kept thinking about my testicles lying in a bloody heap outside of the vasectomy parlor or room or whatever it was. Or, I'd think about speaking in a falsetto voice and taking up knitting as a new hobby. Any way you sliced it (ouch! - pun intended) this was going to be an abysmal experience. Little did I know at the time that abysmal would be the upside compared to what the experience actually turned out to be.

There was a three week lag between when we saw the doc and when the surgery was actually performed. Each day I couldn't help but think a little bit more about this upcoming experience. I would somewhat liken it to a condemned man getting closer to his time in the electric chair. It was seat-squirming, "oh my God", gut check time.

A couple of days before the big event some of the more sensitive guys at work came by and presented me with a gift. I took the wrapping paper off it and bursted out laughing. There was a plain cardboard box with the words "home vasectomy kit" scribbled across it. I opened the box and discovered a soldering iron and some steel clips. The guys that gave it to me laughed like hell as I opened it. Personally, it raised my squeamish quotient up yet another couple of notches. I did appreciate the effort those guys put forward, but at this point, I was finding less and less humor regarding this upcoming experience.

Time went on by and it was soon Vasectomy Eve. Terry Gagnon, our EEO/Affirmative Action Manager, was visiting the plant. Terry and I had dinner that evening and I probably didn't hear over five words that Terry spoke to me because I was so preoccupied about my upcoming surgery. Terry mentioned that he needed to get out to the airport at about seven am the next morning. I told Terry I would run him out to the airport and then it would be time for me to report to the Coliseum Park Hospital to get my balls pasteurized.

I went to bed that night but it was totally pointless - I couldn't sleep. It was probably the most anxiety that I have ever suffered over anything in my life. I tossed and turned and thought about this thing over and over. It had almost (notice I said almost) gotten to the point where the surgery itself would be anticlimactic after all the build-up

I had given it in my mind.

I got up about 5:30 am. Game day! I read the newspaper and watched a little TV. As stated, I'd told Terry I would pick him up around seven o'clock and run him out to the airport. I did this - Terry talked to me a lot on the way but again I didn't acknowledge half of what he said. I hope Terry understood that it had nothing to do with him. I think he knew this - if anything he probably was trying to help divert me from thinking about the festivities at hand.

We got to the airport and Terry got out and went into the terminal. I turned my truck back towards the Williams' Estate and went home. I was going to pick Debbie up and then proceed on to the hospital.

I got to the house and Deb's mom and dad were there. They were going to take the kids home with them for the weekend so that I would have a chance to rest and recuperate from my upcoming trauma. I stood around and talked with them for a few minutes. In fact, to my father-in-law's credit, he tried very hard to be understanding through this thing. He accomplished this with comments like, "I'm glad as hell it ain't me!" or, "Bet you won't go dancing anytime soon!" After these tender words, I was approaching basket case status as my crotch realignment got nearer and nearer. There comes a point when you have to accept the inevitable and this was the point I had now reached. Ready to get it over with - or so I thought.

Deb and I got in the car and headed out towards the hospital. We arrived there about ten til' nine. We checked in and they put us in this little sitting room area that was at the end of a real long hallway. To me, this hallway represented what the condemned see when they walk that last mile - a long, lonely trek. I told Debbie, who was trying to make me feel better, "You can empathize with me all you want to, but when they call my name I'm the one that has to go." Now don't get me wrong - I wasn't trying to be cruel to Debbie. Lord knows, she ought to get a medal just for putting up with me. It's just that people can empathize with you about something until the sun goes down, but, if you are the one that's affected then there's only so far that empathy can go. You have to undergo it, and no one else can quite feel the same way you do about it.

Nine o'clock came and went. It got to be nine oh-five, nine-ten, nine- fifteen, etc. Still no Dr. Fletcher. I thought to myself that he's probably the typical University of Georgia doctor - he's been out drinking all night and I am scheduled to be his first surgery of the day. I could clearly envision him botching the surgery and my mangled member getting tossed into the scrap heap or wherever they toss severed dinguses. A concerned but kind Dr. Fletcher saying to Debbie, "We're so sorry about what happened. Due to technical difficulties beyond our control Ed no longer has a penis. But cheer up! You won't have to ever purchase prophylactics again and he'll stay out of your hair too! In fact, all he'll want to do is watch TV and hum mood music!"

Nine-twenty and twenty-five go by. At this point, I'm pacing. And pacing and pacing. It seemed like time itself was standing still. Finally, at about nine thirty, a nurse comes down the long hallway to get me.

"Mr. Williams?" she asked.

"Yes", I cleverly replied.

"Are you ready for your procedure?" queried the nurse.

"I'll never be ready but let's get it over with." I said.

With that she led me up this long hallway. We then went through a couple of side aisle ways and stepped inside a doorway into a small anteroom. From this anteroom, the nurse opened the door that led into the room where my procedure would be performed.

I walked in and started scoping this room out. It probably measured roughly twenty by twenty-five feet. There was a large countertop with a sink and a bunch of medical supplies arranged on it. A large loudspeaker was bolted up over in one of the corners of the ceiling. There was also a large fluorescent light fixture that was mounted in the center of the ceiling. In the middle of this room, the center piece, the place where my dissection would take place, the examination/ surgical table - awaited me. I stood there, somewhat mutely for a few seconds, drinking this all in. Then I noticed that there were two nurses in the room with me.

Remember when I said earlier that I had some concern over being in this room partially naked with nurses present? That I might get overcome with lust and get erect and want to do vile and lustful things to them? Remember when I said that? I had no need to worry - these women each had to be at least seventy years old and weighed over a couple of hundred pounds apiece as well. They would not have aroused erotic thoughts in San Quentin Prison, much less with me. And besides, even if the Dallas Cowboy's cheerleaders had been there, it wouldn't have mattered at this point. In all my years I don't think I have ever been more afraid. Wild and passionate sex with anyone was definitely the last thing on my mind.....

"Mr. Williams," Old Nurse Number One said.

"Yes mam?"

"Drop your pants and get up on this table." Old Nurse Number one ordered.

"On this little table, mam?" I stammered out.

"Of course on this table, Mr. Williams." she replied.

I slowly unbuckled my belt. I just could not believe the damn indignity of this situation. Doctors grabbing your dick, old nurses telling you to take it all off. It was just too much. But I still found enough self-pride or motivation or whatever to proceed to unhook my belt.

Next I had to unsnap my pants. My first thoughts were - the underwear. Did I remember to use good, new underwear (which was uncomfortable) as opposed to some of my pairs of good old reliable (filled with holes) underwear? (Another thought- why do we call one underwear a pair?) As I unzipped my britches I was pleased to notice that I had some new drawers on. I felt much better so I slowly dropped my pants to my knees and started to step out of them.

"What are you doing Mr. Williams?" inquired Old Nurse Number Two.

"Taking my pants off mam."

"You don't need to take them off, you just need to drop them to your ankles and get up on this table." Old Nurse Number Two explained.

Okay, so this experience was to be the equivalent of a blow job purchased on Cherry Street. Drop your pants to your ankles and get up on the table? I was aghast, but, not so aghast that I didn't do as I was told. I got up there. Tell you the truth, Old Nurses Number One and Two did not look like the sort of ladies you'd want to trifle with. So they gave the orders and I marched......

After lying down upon the table the first things I noticed were the ceiling tiles. I actually sort of studied them for a couple of minutes.

Why, I don't know. Maybe it was some kind of defense mechanism triggered by my brain. You know, diverting yourself using anything available to escape the matter at hand. I had probably been staring at those tiles a few seconds when Old Nurse Number One asked me how many children I had...

"Two", I answered.
"How old are they?" she then asked.
"Five and two", I said.

It really hit me then as to the absurdity of this whole situation. Here I am, thirty-three years old, holder of a responsible job and the father of two kids, lying on a lab table with my dick hanging out, and talking to two old women. I just kept telling myself that this whole ordeal would soon be over with and that the ends would justify the means.

We kept talking, Old Nurses One and Two and I, for about ten or fifteen minutes. Then, Old Nurse Number One said, "let's go ahead and prep him." I didn't know what being prepped meant, but, when I saw Old Nurse Number Two hold up a disposable razor my legs began shaking. "What are you gonna do with that?" I stammered.

"Shave your scrotum so that Dr. Fletcher can perform the surgery." Old Nurse Number Two said. "Please be careful", I whimpered, "Ya'll cannot imagine how I feel right now!" "We can not only imagine it Ed, but, we could feel for ourselves if we wanted to." Old Nurse One said and then started laughing like crazy. I took this to be perverted operating room humour.

I laid as still as I ever have in my life. Actually, in fairness, Old Nurse Number Two did a good job shaving me - I didn't feel anything. But it still was embarrassing. However, I had no time to dwell on this latest in a series of indignities....

Old Nurse Number Two looked up and said she was finished. Then, Old Nurse Number One said that it was time to attach the monitor. I didn't really get too shook up over this comment. I figured the monitor was little more than something similar to the thing they put on your arm to check your blood pressure. I laid there comfortably when.....

"AHHHHHHHHHHHHHHHHHHHHHHHHHH!" I screamed. It felt

like my left leg was on fire! It hurt and stung like mortal hell! I lurched up and saw this big, blue, overly large Band-Aid looking thing adhered to my thigh. I didn't even try to hold the words back.

"What in the hell are you doing to me? What is this damn thing? Are you people sadists?" I hollered.

"Ed, sorry we didn't warn you. This is the monitor used to check your heart and pulse rate while the surgery is being performed," Old Nurse Number Two said.

"What makes it sting so much is that it is soaked in alcohol which makes it very cold to the touch."

"No shit", I said. "All I need are a few more surprises like this. After that you guys don't have to worry about performing the surgery as I will be dead."

"You know Ed," Old Nurse Number Two said, "we may as well get along because we're stuck with each other for the next twenty minutes or so."

I told these two ladies that I meant no offense by anything I'd said, but, that I was scared out of my mind over having to get a vasectomy and that the series of events I had been exposed to thus far had done nothing to improve my mental state. They told me they understood that it was traumatic for a man to go through this but then I got the spiel about women going through childbirth, and how rough it is, and how good it was for me to do this for Debbie, etc. I know that childbirth is traumatic and I would never equate a vasectomy to that but ITS MY DICK AND THIS ALREADY HURTS LIKE HELL AND I HAVEN'T EVEN HAD THE SURGERY YET! That's what I wanted to yell out but I was afraid I would embarrass Debbie with the noise so I sort of weakly smiled at the old biddies and prayed for this to all be over with.

We small-talked for a few more minutes and then a message came through the speaker, "Dr. Fletcher has been tied up in surgery. It will be thirty to forty-five minutes before he'll be here."

Old Nurse Number Two walked over to where I was lying and said, "No reason for you to hang around here. We'll come back and get you when Doc Fletcher arrives."

With that, Old Nurse Number Two reaches over and rips the monitor off my thigh. Now, when I say rips, I mean rips! That thing had a ton of adhesive on it so that when she ripped it off I damn near came up off the table. I mean, I don't have a lot of hair on top of my head but I do have a ton on my legs and when she pulled this blue thing off it hurt - BAD!

I couldn't get my britches up and get out of that room quickly enough. I halfway sprinted down the hall to where Debbie was. She asked me, "Are you through?" I proceeded to tell her about what had happened and that I had not even got started yet. She couldn't believe it - I chimed in at this point with the thought that maybe this just wasn't meant to be and that we should just go on home.

"No - we've made the appointment and have gotten this far so let's just calm down and get it over with." Debbie stated. I never argue with Debbie - it's like Forrest Gump and Jenny, if she tells me to do something I do it. So, I guessed I'd be staying and having this surgery done. I did notice that during the period that I was again in the waiting area that another couple walked up and joined us. The male of the couple piped up......

"Having the big V done, huh?" he said.
"Yeah, looks that way." I cleverly replied.
"You seem to be a little bit nervous about it." Jim (as he later told me what his name was) astutely said.
"Why would you say that?"
"Well Ed, I couldn't help but overhear some of ya'lls conversation. I also couldn't help but notice that you have just about worn this carpet out from pacing back and forth."

Jim was right as I had probably covered a couple of miles on that carpet since returning from the Pit of Horrors. In fact, I have always been one of those types that's fidgety as hell all the time. I stay in perpetual motion until I drop off to sleep. There are a few good things about this quality though. I seem to have a lot of energy, which gets me through work and the kids and stuff. The negative is that it would sure be nice to be able to relax a little more than I do. Anyway, to get back to the story, Jim did make an astute observation regarding the pacing.

Jim and Sheila asked Debbie and I how old we were and how

many kids we had and other more personal type questions. This was starting to chafe me a little bit. Now, I know that both of us are there to get our groins severed - I happened to be going first and Jim was going second. But this soon-to-be shared experience did not entitle them to quiz Debbie and me about our personal lives. Since this teed me off, I figured the best comeback was to start enlightening Jim a little about my experiences minutes earlier in the operating room. I told him all about the last hour, in as vivid detail as I could. As this charming story leaked out, I noted that his face got a little pale. To compensate for this, he began teasing me more about my continual pacing in the hallway.

"Damn Ed, you're acting like you're about to walk the last mile." Jim intoned.

"No Jim, I'm just stepping up my aerobic conditioning program here at the hospital." I sarcastically replied.

"No reason to be hostile, Ed." Jim replied.

I really didn't give a damn what Jim nor any other human being thought of me at this point - I was mentally as close to collapse as I have ever been. This time being spent waiting for the doctor——it was going by soooo slow. Finally, after I had walked about fourteen miles pacing on the carpet back and forth, Old Nurse Number Two came back down the hall.

"Hon, Doc Fletcher is here. Hitch 'em up and let's go."

(I don't know quite what she meant by that but) I went quietly up the hall with her. I did turn around to give Debbie the most pitiful look I could muster. I guess I was thinking that I was never going to see her again as a fully functioning man. One other interesting thing that I noted as I went up the hall was that bastard Jim suddenly quieted down and looked as if someone had cursed him with the mark of the pentagram or something. I think he was really starting to feel the pressure of being next. It was the only glimmer of satisfaction that I would get until this ordeal was over.

We went through all the same hallways that I mentioned earlier. I was really sort of numb at this and ready to be done with this. So ready that when I stepped in the operating room I dropped my britches without being asked and laid down on the table. Old Nurses One and Two didn't say too much as they had already experienced significant on-line time viewing my exposed member earlier. Ole Doc Fletcher was talking to me about how sorry he was about being late. I, of course, told him it was no big deal which, of course, is one of the bigger lies I've ever told.

Doc went on to talk to me about sports and other related stuff. Now, I'm not a kid - I fully realize that he is trying to take my mind off what is about to occur. And I don't blame him for that. The only thing is, short of a fifty million dollar lotto jackpot win, nothing was going to take my mind off the festivities that were about to occur.

Reality reared its ugly head when Doc said, "Razor!" Now, that was comforting! I stammered out, "Doc, what's the need for a razor?" Doc replied, "Ed, before I can do the surgery I need to get rid of a little more pubic hair."

Old Nurses One and Two looked pretty severe as the doc was basically saying that they didn't do a complete job of shaving me. All I could do was brace myself for the cold steel that was coming yet again. Actually the doc came over, deftly lifted my member up (for some strange reason there was no erotic sensation at all), and began shaving. To his credit, I hardly felt anything. The only problem was that my dreading of being shaved again made the anticipation of the "main event" that much worse......

Well, when he got my weenie as hairless as the day I was born, ole Doc Fletcher told me that the moment of truth had arrived. It was time to begin the surgery. I asked the Doc what was next in the sequence of steps that would end with my neuterization.

"Ed, we've got to administer some anesthetic so that there will be no pain." said Doc.

Now, that was cool. I was already feeling better! Ole Doc Fletcher would administer some morphine or some other hallucinogen that would cause me not to feel pain even if I was on the receiving end of a shark attack. This moment of comfort lasted only until Doc Fletcher said, "Ed, you realize that we're going to have to give you a local directly in the scrotum".

A local directly in the scrotum?!!! My God! A needle into my bag of pleasure? It was too horrible to even think about!

Horrible or not I felt an intense stinging pain where I had never felt one before. Ole' Doc was wasting no time with this operation. It hurt so badly that tears came to my eyes. Of course, the first thought I had was to get the hell up and get out. But it hit me - am I gonna get up with a needle in my card sack? I don't think so... Gory thoughts hit me regarding my jumping up from the table and me tearing my balls from my body. No way that can happen man - I would've laid there if Richard Simmons had come into the room with a pink tutu on and carrying some flowers for me. I couldn't move! I had to trust this bastard from Georgia to deal with the most important part of my body.

Finally the needle was removed - and was I relieved! Relieved until the Doc told me that it would take yet two more shots before there was enough anesthetic for the surgery to be performed. Damned if he didn't reload the needle and jab it into the ole' scrot yet again.

God, did it hurt! I thought at the very least that the second jab would not hurt quite as badly as the first one did. Wrong again! It hurt and it hurt bad. I actually began to relax at this point because I thought the shots were over with. This turned out to be one of the stupidest assumptions I ever made. The reason it was so stupid was because the Doc then shot me three more times on the right side! Three! By the fifth one, I just didn't care anymore. Remember when I wrote earlier about how hyper I am, and how much energy it gives me, and all the other good stuff that goes along with it? One of the bad characteristics associated with it is that it takes a lot of anesthetic to put me under, or numb me, or whatever. That's why I don't really drink much - it takes a lot of booze for me to get a buzz going, and the effect goes away really fast.

Back to the shots - once the Doc was through making a pin cushion out of the right side of my scrotum he turned his attention to the left. "Ed", said Doc, "these shots shouldn't be nearly as bad as the others." "Right you old bastard!" I wanted to say but dared not because of the fact that I was lying on this table with my genitals exposed to a man with a knife in his hand. Hell, I would've probably even rooted for the University of Georgia at that point if he had asked me to. In any event, he was right - these shots were not quite as bad. I ended up taking about three more shots in the left side. The only positive thing that came out of this is that I learned that your dinglebag can take a lot more abuse than you think it can.

Once the shots were completed the ole Doc sharpened up his scapel. "Ed, I'm going to make a slight incision to begin this surgery. Should you feel any pain please let me know." I thought that a simple shriek or wail would accomplish this and I told the Doc that that was what I intended to do. He laughed and said, "You're a little nervous about this aren't you?"

I laid there deathly still and continued looking up at the ceiling. I counted holes in the ceiling tiles, thought about work, and just generally tried to think about anything that could hold interest for me. Nothing worked. I drifted about in this state until the sharp pulling sensation in my right testicle brought tears to my eyes. I still didn't move...

"Just pulling the right tube out, cutting a section off, and cauterizing both ends of it, Ed." Doc Fletcher said. I couldn't help but blurt out, "Dammit, Doc! I don't want to know what you're doing to me! You're killing me!" I shouted.

"Sorry, Ed, you're still a little squeamish over this thing aren't you?" Doc said for about the tenth time.

I cleverly replied, "I really am Doc, but I have a lot of faith in your abilities." What a crock that was but if you think I was gonna do anything to piss this man off then you have judged me wrong. I would've told him he could play the guitar like Randy Bachman if it would've gotten me out of there alive.

The hot, intense pain from having my cord severed subsided as the Doc sewed the right side up. He then turned his attentions to my left side. This time the cuts were no so bad as I had about a quart of anesthetic floating around in my scrotum. Still, I felt a little tug as he tuned my strings on the left side.....

Suddenly the doc looks over at me and says, "It's over, Ed." I couldn't have been happier if Elvis himself had entered the operating room with his band and began a concert! I profusely thanked the Doc and old Nurses One and Two. I then asked the Doc if I could go home. He nodded his approval, and I got up, ready to leave.

As I came up off the operating table I did so very stiffly (sort of like how Frankenstein came up off the lab table in those old horror movies). I wondered why I was so stiff and it hit me that I was trying to do as little as possible to affect myself "down there". There was a good reason for this. Ed Jr. had told me earlier of a little episode with a friend of his at the gas plant. Apparently this guy goes in for a vasectomy. When its done, he ignores the doctor's instructions to take it easy for a few days - he mows grass, lifts things, and even (and I do find this hard to believe) claimed to have had sex with his wife that very same day. The result of all this was that his genitalia turned a very bright purple color and stayed that way for several weeks! There was no way that I was going to have the genitals of hell - mine were going to be well taken care of. And also, for some strange reason, I had this irrational fear that my balls were going to fall off. I guess I felt that the incisions Doc Fletcher had made were huge (they were actually about one quarter of an inch long) and that if I didn't exercise extreme care my balls would fall off and roll down the street. In this spirit I got up off the table and stood - I was a little shaky but essentially okay. The first thing the Doc and the Old Nurses did after I stood was hand me something called a suspensory. A suspensory, for those of you not in the know, is a device that is nothing more than an elastic strap with a pouch in it. This strap goes around your waist and your balls go in the pouch. It's sort of an after-vasectomy jock strap. What I did was put it on and cinch it up just as tight as I could. I wanted my balls to be as immobile as I could get them. Once this was done, I asked Old Nurse Number 2 to hand me my pants from the floor. She asked me why I didn't pick them up myself? I told her that under no circumstances was I going to bend over and that it was the least she could do after spending almost an hour viewing my privates (you know you can say what you will but any profession where you stare at other people's genitalia for hours requires a somewhat kinky, don't-give-a-damn type person). I was really concerned that I would somehow damage myself if I bent over and grabbed my pants. Actually, Old Nurse Number 2 looked somewhat amused by my request (the first time that I had seen her smile that day) and picked up the belt part of my pants and handed them to me. I tucked my shirt in, zipped my zipper, and headed for the door.

As it turned out, Old Nurse Two guided me away from the operating room, through some doors, and out into the main hallway. As for me, I was walking somewhat like Grandpa McCoy - very hesitatingly, step by tortuous step. I continued to not want to do anything that would cause my genitalia to move or bounce.

We got to the intersection part of the hallway that I mentioned to you earlier. Here we stopped. Old Nurse Number Two looked down the hall to the right and lo and behold, way down there at the end was Debbie. I had forgotten in the midst of all these events that that she was there. As soon as Debbie saw us she immediately came up the hall. I was real glad to see her because all I wanted to do was get the hell out of that hospital. Debbie, I'm sure, was as anxious as I was to get out and to commit this experience to our past.

As Debbie approached me I noticed another person hot on her heels - in fact, if Debbie had stopped walking I think he would've run right into her. As Debbie and this guy came closer I saw that it was my good friend Jim! It appeared now though that Jim was somewhat paler and not near as sure of himself as he was when we'd talked earlier. This was a far cry from the annoying, cocky individual that had gotten so amused over my nervousness just a short while ago.

Debbie walked up and gave me the most pitiful look that she has ever given me. I knew that she was feeling sorry for me, and frankly, I was content to let her feel that way. There was a little of this "feel sorry for myself" attitude shining through - although how I could feel that way was interesting as Debbie did give birth to two children and went through far more pain than I ever have, or will. I was very tired and just wanted to go home.

This pleasant interlude was interrupted by Jim, who got right up in my face and with a pale and quivery voice asked, "How was it Ed?" I couldn't help but lower the boom, "Jim", I barely whispered, "it was one of the worst experiences of my life." Jim's face appeared to lose about a quart of blood. "Damn, Ed, was it that bad?" Jim asked as the tremble in his voice became more pronounced. "Jim, it was the needle that made it awful." I said in a voice that sounded like I was getting ready to cry. "NEEDLE?" Jim blurted. "Yeah Jim - they have to stick the needle with the anesthetic directly into one of your testicles. It goes in a good half inch."

I swear to God that his face became almost blue. Before he could say anything else, Old Nurse Two grabbed him by the arm and started escorting him down the hall. Jim looked like a man who was about to fulfill his destiny with the electric chair. Debbie asked me, in a low voice, "Why did you tell him that? Did they really stick the needle in your you-know-whats?" I told Debbie, "Of course not, but he deserved it. Besides who are you concerned about, him or me?" That really helped me as it diverted Debbie's attention from the injustice I had just done Jim, and got the sympathy quotient for me skyrocketing upwards again.

I did my best Frankenstein walk from the hospital out to the car. Debbie held the door open for me and even helped me into our vehicle. Once we were both inside, I implored Debbie not to drive real fast nor to do anything that would cause vibration in the car. I especially asked her not to accidentally hit a pothole or drive over some railroad tracks on the way home.

We cruised down the highway and got closer to our house. By this point I was hurt, tired, and emotionally exhausted by the entire experience. A few miles from the house we did strike a small pothole, which got me a little closer to God, and finally we got home as our car pulled into the driveway.

Our car slowed to a stop. I staggered out and was greeted by my father-in-law, who was standing at the door. He had the most concerned look on his face that I've ever seen him have. "Are you okay, boy?" he asked. I just sort of gave him a wan sort of smile and said, "I've seen better days." With that, I went into the house and headed for the bedroom.

Once inside the bedroom I shut the door. The first order of business was to take a shower and lie down. I had brought a stack of work home with me so having something to do over the weekend would not be a problem. I slowly and methodically took off my clothes. It probably took me fifteen minutes to do it because I was so careful. Then, I uncinched the suspensory and walked as slowly into the bathroom as I ever have in my life. I swear that in my delirium I was thinking that my cardsack had been severed and that any sudden movement would cause it to fall off. I then got into the shower and turned the hot water on. It felt really good as it hit my dismembered body. I stood there and soaked for awhile and then got up the courage to look down and examine the mutilations that had just occurred. In looking down at the ol' scrot I found that the incisions were extremely tiny (about a quarter of an inch as I mentioned earlier). In fact, so tiny that they were sort of hard to find. I was starting to feel a little bit better about this. Then, I reluctantly got out of the shower and very carefully put on sleep pants, a T-shirt, and a robe. The main reason for the robe was that I was going to sit down on the bed, lean against the headboard, and do the work that I just mentioned. While doing this work an icebag would be resting against my scarred genitalia. I didn't want Deb or her mom or Alison or someone else to walk into the room and see me sitting there with an ice bag up against my you-know-whats. Debbie and her mom would understand but Alison might talk about this in Sunday School or something. The best course of action, it seemed, was to go with the robe.

Back to the story - I sat up on the bed and began writing and reading some of the documents that I had brought home. It didn't take long for the combination of work, lack of sleep, and general fatigue to cause me to nap. I was halfway asleep when I noticed a blur out of the corner of my eye. In fact, a blur that was coming straight towards me! Opening my eyes I saw that Alison had run into the room and had jumped in the air with the intention of landing in my lap! The only thing I could do was catch her in the air and deposit her on the other side of the bed. This move resembled the powerslam maneuver that many pro wrestlers use. Anyway, Alison's landing was quite soft but my flipping her over on the other side of the bed scared her and she began to cry. "Why you throw Alison, Dad?" she asked. I replied, "Daddy hurt himself and if you had landed on him he would be going to the cemetery." Alison said, "I don't want you to go there so it's okay." I felt better, she felt better, and that was the end of it.

That basically ends this chapter but I do feel the need to make a few closing comments:

First off, and this is directed at any man who is reading this, don't dare believe this hooey about how painless and effortless vasectomies are - it's a crock! A vasectomy is one of the most harrowing experiences that a man will ever go through. The pain and humiliation involved in the procedure, coupled with the general uncertainty as to what's going on, assures that. But, I think in spite of all this, that it's the right thing to do. Women do go through far more than we men do when they have children - our children. Since they go through this it only seems fair that the man takes care of his end of the bargain. And think about this - do you really want to take the chance of finding out that you're to be a father at age forty-eight? Not me pal - I'd get vasectomies every day before I would choose that option.

Secondly, the humiliation does not end after the surgery is done. There is one more part of this experience called the post-operative check-up that needs to be discussed. Basically what this is is that you have to go back each couple of weeks after the surgery and submit "a sample" to the doctor until he/she assures you that your sperm count is zero. This has to be done because right after the surgery you'll still have some live sperm cells swimming around in your system. There's been more than one couple along the way who started having unprotected sex right after the vasectomy and were rewarded with another baby for their efforts. You obviously don't want this to happen, so, you have to submit a sample. Modesty forbids me to detail the anguish of having to procure the sample so we'll go right into the next step in the "sampling" process - submitting it to the urologist.

Submitting the sample takes the concept of total humiliation one step further. You get a jar, typically a baby food jar or something similar, and deposit a sample in it (yuck!). Then you have to take it by the doctor's office. I can remember wanting to wear a disguise when I took my first sample in. And be advised here that you may have to take in several before you get a clean bill of health. And what do you do in the meantime? Well, if in the meantime includes sex you may as well get ready to visit the ugly girls at X-Mart and buy some prophylactics (the joys of this experience are fully detailed in chapter 8, item 15). This is, as explained before, an exhilarating experience for the married man. Thankfully though, on around the second or third pass through the doctor's office you'll get a clean bill of sexual health. You are officially shooting blanks. This does give you the right to have unprotected sex with the wife (although by eliminating the possibility of unwanted pregnancy and disease the filthy, seamy side of sex is removed and therefore some of the fun). It also gives you the right to hang around the rubbers rack at X-Mart and laugh at those who still have to purchase prophylactics. It also invites your spouse to ponder the question as to was it a wise move to get you sterilized when it means that you could have sex with someone and not have to worry about getting them pregnant. As I told Debbie one day when she made this point, the odds that I would pursue someone else in the day of AIDS and herpes is pretty minimal. This leads us to the third point.....

The third point is that you can use this experience to get a lot of gratuitous sex. This is the way you do it - about a week or so after the vasectomy, you start to feel the desire to have sex again. You'll need to immediately inform the wife of this. The reason for informing her is that she'll let you have the first shot just out of sympathy. And make no mistake about it - sex is sex! I don't care whether it happens because of passion, guilt, recreational needs, athletic needs, or whatever other things compel us. Remember, again, sex is sex. So, take the first post-vasectomy plunge with the pride of a man who knows they have undergone genital mutilation for the experience. Enjoy, enjoy, enjoy!

After you submit your first "sample" to the urologist just go to your wife and calmly say (with a straight face), "The doctor looked at my sample and I'm still potent. The only thing that's going to get the sperm cells out of my system is very frequent sexual relations so that they are purged out." This works every time - the need to get away from the chance of pregnancy coupled with the opportunity to not have to use birth control devices will get the wife to come through for you whenever you desire! In fact, this is the only time in the marriage, other than the honeymoon, where you'll be allowed to have so much sex on a frequent basis. Utilize the opportunity to its fullest! (A derivative of the same scheme can be used when you're trying to get pregnant with the first child. Look at your wife calmly and say, "Look, all this stuff about checking your temperature or timing the number of days or whatever else people say to do to have a child is a bunch of crap. If we're really interested there is only one proven method of success - we need to have sex every day for the next cycle of days! It will be tough, and there'll be days when we won't want to do it, but we must fortify ourselves and go through with it for the sake of our future family!" I used this technique twice and it worked quite well - we had two beautiful children and I had two of the happiest months of my life. If you don't believe it works - try it! You'll definitely be glad you did!

Now to conclude guys, aren't you glad you read this? I felt like it was time that the real truth about the vasectomy procedure be disseminated to all American males. Please feel free to use this information as you see fit and if you happen to stop by a X-Mart and you're lonely, just wink at one of the check-out girls. They'll take it from there......

CHAPTER 14

THE ADULTERY BUSINESS

You know, I truly believe that America is the land of opportunity. I've listened time and time again to success stories that come from many ordinary Americans. These Americans come from all over the country and have many varied backgrounds and personal histories. These achievers have started restaurants, car repair places, clothing stores, and many other types of businesses that have done well. More and more business success is attributable to the concept of "niche marketing". Niche marketing, by definition, is quite simple. A little history lesson will explain the significance of it.

Remember years ago when all you had were the three major TV networks? Products were sold based on a broad appeal type of marketing strategy. Features or items that would please select groupings of consumers were ignored for those that would appeal to the masses. When the development level of communication technology was at this point this concept worked well.

In the early eighties cable television really hit its stride. Suddenly channels like CNN, the Nashville Network, USA, Discovery, MTV, and numerous others came on the air with offerings that appealed to niches, or select groups, of people. Because of their success, advertisers found that product offerings could be designed that would appeal to these niches. This concept has led to the growth of many new ideas, products, and services that would have been inconceivable just a few years ago. Items like tennis shoes - remember when tennis shoes were your basic PF Flyers or Keds and came in three colors - red, black, or white, and two styles - low or high tops? Look at the offerings now - you can buy jogging shoes, running shoes, basketball shoes, tennis shoes, shoes with "air" in them, and countless other variations. These products sell well because good marketing research identifies the niches and manufacturing companies produce the products. Supply and demand - one of the most basic business concepts there is.

Now there is one relatively under explored niche in the marketing of products that needs to be exploited. This is the niche containing people that are adulterers. I'm not one to throw stones or cast aspersions on how others live their lives. I look at it like this - I have enough to worry about in leading my own life. I don't worry about how others live theirs. Live and let live. Plus, I don't think in a lot of cases that we bother to understand why people engage in activities like adultery anyway. So let's leave out the moral issues and concentrate on this important niche market.

Why is this niche important? Well, think about it a second. The statistics show that over half of the marriages in this country end up in divorce. And one of the main reasons for these divorces is adultery. To be conservative, let's say that half of the divorces are caused by one or both of the marital partners committing adultery. If our assumption is true then there's a big market out there for products or services aimed at adulterers. I mean, think about the business possibilities..........

Motels for adulterers only - this could really catch on. Offerings like: no phone calls forwarded into the room for any reason, security in the parking lot that would only let adulterers or about-to-be adulterers in, pamphlets that give you one hundred and one good reasons that you and the wife are not getting along, fake ID/driver's license services, bellmen and front desk personnel taught not to smirk and to treat the couple as married, fencing around the parking lot that doesn't allow the cars inside to be seen, etc., etc. Instead of the traditional fruit basket in the room, niceties like exotic bath oils, strong mouthwashes, and appropriate birth control devices could be offered.

This thing could really take off and go with the right entrepreneur behind it. In fact, I would suggest the name "Strays Inn" for the motel chain itself.

Restaurants for adulterers- this could be a hot ticket as well. Waiters could be instructed never to admit knowing either member of the couple (even if he had waited on them, with different partners, four hundred times before), silverware would have fingerprints removed when cleaned, restrooms would offer items like birth control devices and mouthwash and stuff that would clean lipstick off collars, and place settings could   have slogans on them like, "With love, there is no shame." The possibilities are endless. Proposed name for this restaurant chain, "Lies, Thighs, and Fries."

Private Investigators Who Back Up the Story of the Guilty Party - This alone, done properly, would enable the entrepreneur to become as wealthy as Bill Gates. Think of how much the caught spouse would be willing to pay to prove that they didn't commit the dirty deed? Think of how much you'd be willing to part with to have the investigator, with a straight face and professional attitude, refute all of your spouse's allegations. Why, you could build in a fee structure that was say, equal to what your first six months of alimony payments would've been. It's a natural. Proposed name for this business, "Straight Faces Detective Agency."

I could go on with more ideas like these but you get my point. Businesses targeted at this market could make billions. But, let's stop for a second because I want to make the following assertion - there are already businesses reaping the rewards in this lucrative niche market! There really are - and the first business I will mention to you might be a surprise (obviously it will be to around fifty percent of you, give or take a percentage point).

Ever heard of the cruise business? You know, those ships that take people all over the world to lots of exotic places? Well, one of their major revenue sources is the adulterers market! That's correct - the adulterers market! You may think that this is a totally unfounded assertion but there's a lot of truth to it. To get to the bottom of my assertion, let me relate a true story to you.......

A few months ago Ron Miller and I became aficionados of the Jerky Boys. You know those guys that make the prank phone calls and then record them? They've sold millions of tapes/CD's and there's a reason for it. First, the calls they record are absolutely real - they're not staged. Secondly, these guys do good impersonations of foreign people, gay people, rednecks, etc. Ron and I listened to some of their stuff at lunch one day and we were marveling at how these guys made all this $$$$ by making prank phone calls. Of course, as was our wont, somewhere in the conversation one of us made the brilliant observation that we had as much talent as the Jerky Boys did. From that aside we quickly decided that we should make a couple of these calls ourselves to prove our talents.

That afternoon, which happened to be a Friday, Ron and I decided to make a "Jerky Boys" call. I turned the speakerphone on so that the conversation could be heard by both of us. Then, I dialed a local travel agency.

The phone rang several times and then a pleasant sounding lady answered it. "Hello", she said, "Ajax Travel Agency, my name is Maggie. Can I help you?" "Yes", I said in a gruff voice, "I need to talk to somebody there about a quick trip to the Bahamas." "Yes sir, I think we can help you with that", this lady sweetly intoned. "What sort of plans do you have?"

I thought for a second. "Miss", I said, "My name is Frank. Frank Robinson." "Yes Mr. Robinson, very nice to talk with you. My name is Pam", she replied. "Nice to meet you Pam. Now's here's what I need. I wanna leave for the Bahamas Friday. Come back Sunday. Got anything like that?" Pam paused for a second and replied, "Why yes, I think we do, let me go into the computer and look." "Hurry up, I ain't got all day." I loudly replied.

A few minutes go by. "Mr. Robinson, I found something on Smithereen's Cruise Lines that fits your criteria." "That's good there Miss', I said, "But I have another question?" "What is your question, sir?" Pam asked. "Just how discreet are these ships?" I queried.

There was silence for several moments. "Discreet sir? I'm afraid I don't understand what you mean?" Pam stammered out.

"What I mean is this, Toots - I'm gonna be taking someone I can have fun with on this cruise, not my wife, get me? And I wanna be damn sure that I don't run into somebody I know while I'm on this ship." After that was said there was silence on the other end.

"Look", I went on, "I know you don't probably approve of what I'm doing. But this little blonde really makes me feel good. And I'm tired of doing what I'm supposed to all the time. Now, I'm concerned about how discreet this ship is. Can you give me a passenger list?"

Another fairly lengthy period of silence went by - finally Pam said, "Sir, I can't get access to a passenger list. The cruise company won't give them out. Anyway, the chances that you'll run into someone you know on the ship are pretty slim."

At this point, I had to hit the mute button on the phone so that Ron and I could get some laughter out of our systems I hit the button again, went live, and asked Pam, "Can you guarantee I won't run into someone I know?"

Pam politely replied, "Of course not, sir. However, we can put you and your friend in an out-of-the-way cabin, thus lessening the chance of your being observed."

I was starting to feel a little guilty about putting Pam through all this. I thanked her for all her hard work regarding this matter. Then I said, "I hope you don't think badly of me for taking someone other than my wife on this cruise."

Pam replied, "Don't apologize - I don't pass judgments on other people. Plus, I'd say that HALF of our business comes from people with needs like yours!"

Can you believe it? Half of the people that book cruises through this travel agency are practicing adulterers! Half! I mean why should we really be surprised? In this era of niche marketing? Hell, the cruise business is one of the first to wise up and cater to this rich and ever growing niche! And you can't blame the cruise lines because they're only providing a service that the public desires. After this experience, I can't help but laugh anytime I see a cruise line ad - I wonder what percentage of passengers are strolling along on the decks deliriously happy cause they're having fun with someone other than their spouses? Can you imagine what the condom vending machines on these ships gross? Hell, I'll bet that the prophylactic companies probably have a majority stockholder interest in some of these cruise lines. It wouldn't surprise me at all.

I don't have a whole lot more to say about this particular subject - I sort of stumbled into it through this prank phone call and was surprised at what I found out. It seems that the adulterers market, like many others, has more than enough willing vendors that are ready and able to cater to its particular needs. So adulterers, there is hope. Keep on sailin'. 'Nuff said.

CHAPTER 15

DOG

Sometimes things happen in your life that make you really sit back and think. Think about what the important things in life are and what they aren't. Think about your life, what it means, what you want it to be, and what it has been. Think about those close to you and why they should be cherished. For so few people are really worth expending true emotion and feeling and commitment on....

I just returned from a funeral. We buried Dog today. Debbie, Will, and I went (Alison had an art class) along with over three hundred other people. That's right - over three hundred other people. The obvious question is, "Who, or what, was Dog?"

Dog was my uncle Jimmy. Jimmy was the third oldest child that Ed Sr. and Lillian (Miss Lily) produced. In order, there was Ed Jr., Franklin, Jimmy, Jerry, Robert, and Lorena.

One thing a little unusual about the Williams' is that everyone was tagged with a nickname. My dad was "Wolf", Franklin "Jew", Jimmy "Dog", Jerry "Calhoun", Robert "Lil Brother", and Lorena "Fee". At Dog's funeral all sorts of people talked with my dad - it was "Wolf this" and "Wolf that". Nobody smiled or laughed when it was said. That's what he's called. Their nicknames are how all of them are referred to by their friends.

In explaining the nicknames, my dad got "Wolf" from the fact that in his younger days he had a shock of blond hair. Along with that went the fact that he was six foot one, weighed about two hundred five pounds, and looked like he was cut from granite. The women loved him and apparently he loved them right back. The "Wolf" label was tagged to him then and is with him to this day.

Franklin, the next uncle, has real dark hair and is slender. Physically, he really doesn't resemble any of his brothers or sister that much. The "Jew" tag came from his dark complexion and general appearance. Don't get me wrong - I have friends who are Jewish and I have a lot of respect for the Jewish people. But this is Franklin's nickname and this is how people who know him refer to him. I haven't heard one laugh or anti-Semitic remark used when they do so.

Jimmy, who came next, got the "Dog" tag because of some of the things he liked to do. You had to understand Dog - he had one of the best, most outgoing personalities that anyone could ask for. You could not help but like him. He was one of those type people that treated everyone the same. This held true whether you were a janitor or the president of IBM. I know my dad cares about his brothers and sister, but Jimmy and he were always the closest of the bunch.

Jimmy, to give one example of why people "nicked" him Dog, loved to fight chickens. The official name for this sport is cockfighting. For many years he had a building way out back in the woods behind his house that he used to fight chickens in. It had a pit (a concrete ring about a foot high with a diameter of about ten to twelve feet) that was used to stage the fights themselves. There were sets of bleachers that surrounded the pit for spectators. Behind the bleachers on one side of the building was a concession stand. From this stand you could buy cokes, beer, potato chips, candy, cigarettes, or whatever. Usually Dog had his daughters (Misti and Elaine) or his wife (Clara) working the concessions. On the other side of the building were the restroom facilities. It was like a small stadium or indoor arena.

On any night that Dog held these fights he could be assured that he would have some local boys enter his tournaments and some out-of-towners as well. Ed Jr. raised chickens at our home and fought them in Dog's tournaments several times over the years. Wayne Smith (aka Coogler, although what this nic means I haven't a clue), who also lives in Juliette and is a good friend of both Ed Jr. and Dog, fought chickens as well.

Cock-fighting (the correct name for this sport although chicken fighting is what I always refer to it as) begins with the roosters having gaffs attached to their legs. Gaffs are leather wraps that are pulled around the chicken's legs and tied. Attached to the gaff is a long metal spike (or spur). After the gaffs are tied on, the roosters are brought to the center of the pit by their handlers. The roosters are then allowed to peck at each other while being held by the handlers. This is done to get the competitive juices of each rooster stimulated. Then, at the referee's signal, the roosters are released and they begin fighting. The fight continues until one rooster kills the other. I know this sounds brutal, and that the animal rights activists out there will go nuts, but that's how it works - the roosters fight until one or the other is killed. Its a very pure example of survival of the fittest.

During the night win-lose records were kept of each handler's roosters and cash prizes were awarded at the end of the evening based on whose "stable" performed the best. Always accompanying these matches was quite a bit of informal betting. It was customary for the men to shout bets across the pit to each other while the matches were going on. Ed Sr. went to these fights often and always seemed to come away with lots of money. The language that was used during the matches was pretty colorful and I got some memorable laughs while attending some of these fights.

One clue as to Dog's popularity with people was the size of these crowds - he would have as many as a hundred or more people attend. Another thing that was interesting was that he would regularly have area law enforcement people at these cockfights! For those of you who are not aware, cockfighting in Georgia is illegal, but Dog regularly had local law enforcement personnel attend these fights and cuss, bet, and laugh along with the rest of us. It was a familial type atmosphere and enjoyed by all who attended.

Around 1976 a movie was filmed at Dog's cockfighting arena called "The Cockfighter". Warren Oates starred in it - I can't remember the basic plot (the movie did poorly in the United States but did much better overseas) but a lot of it was filmed in Juliette using Dog's pit and arena. It was exciting seeing all the movie people and movie equipment used in the making of the film (a scene to be repeated in Juliette fourteen years later when "Fried Green Tomatoes" was filmed there). Many people we knew in Juliette got parts as extras in the movie. Dog got along with all the movie people so well that he was offered and accepted a speaking role in the movie! In fact, the movie people liked him so much that he was offered an opportunity to travel with the movie company and act in more films in the future. Dog turned this opportunity down because he would have been away from his family and Juliette for long stretches of time, and, this he did not want to do. It was really something to see how well Dog mingled with these movie people and how readily they took to him and made him one of them.

Another thing I always liked about Dog was his love of music. He loved that good ole fifties rock 'n' roll and most country music. In fact, in the 1970's the Allman Brothers Band bought and lived on a farm in suburban Juliette. And guess what - Jimmy got to be friends with all the members of the band. He got especially close to Dickie Betts, the lead guitarist for the group. Dog spent many hours at the Allman Brother's Ranch and was so well liked that he had access to it anytime he wanted. He would tell Ed Jr. and Ernest and me many colorful stories about some of the goings-on inside that ranch.

There were advantages to having the Allman Brother's Band living just a few miles from one's house. One distinct advantage was that most evenings you could hear them practice - many of their hits like "Ramblin Man", "Melissa", and others I heard for the first time sitting at the end of my front yard. My brother and I sat out there numerous times and listened to them play. Another advantage to having the Brothers in town was that a continual stream of celebrities was always visiting them. Cher and Paul McCartney were among two of the most notable. Everyone that met Cher felt her to be very down to earth and approachable. And how many of us would have guessed that Paul McCartney would've had a chat with the postmaster in Juliette? One of the funniest episodes that occurred during our celebrity time with the Brothers involved Marvin Bowdoin, Sr. and Gregg Allman. Marvin was a good friend to most everyone in Juliette and ran a combination gas station/laundry mat/restaurant/convenience store. It sits on the corner of the junction between Juliette Road and I-87. One day, after the Brothers first came to town, Gregg Allman was riding his motorcycle down highway 87. As he approached the section of highway where Marvin's store sits, he skidded on some gravel and fell off his motorcycle. A lot of police officers showed up to investigate and to be sure Gregg was all right (he was - no major injuries). Marvin was quite perturbed about the accident and the fact that so many people seemed to be concerned about it. When Ed Jr. walked into Marvin's that morning the accident had just happened and several of the men there were discussing it. One of the guys asked Marvin who had the accident and why there was so much interest in it. Marvin replied, "It was some goddamned hippie. Said his name was Allman!" Then he added, "Why they care so much about the long-haired bastard I don't know!" Which only goes to show that Marvin was a good man but a connoisseur of popular music he was not.

Dog did love the music and loved the outdoors as well. He hunted, fished, and generally just loved to be outside. One time Ed Jr., Dog, Robert, Brother, and I were sitting around shooting the breeze. Dog had just come in from a morning of deer hunting. He said that four other guys had hunted with him and they got in their deer stands about 5:30 am that morning. Around 9:30 am or so they decided to call it a day. They walked through the woods and got to an adjoining cow pasture. Dog begins to hear some loud sounds. At first he can't make these sounds out, but, as the guys keep walking, it becomes clear that the sounds are that of a human. A human voice - a loud, very upset human voice! Hearing curses and screams in the air, Dog and his posse go to investigate.

History books will not note the name of Mootie Johnson (where in the hell the name Mootie came from I don't know and I've never heard of anyone else named that) but I will remember his name until the day I die. For it was Mootie Johnson that Dog and his boys came upon. To be fair, Mootie had an IQ that was probably twenty points lower than Forrest Gump's. Anyway, the tender scene that Dog and the boys found in process was that of Mootie Johnson, pants down around his ankles, makin' whoopee with one of the cows in the pasture. What had Mootie hollering so much was that ole' Bossie, at the moment of highest passion, had dropped a load of cow pies right down on Mootie's britches! For this indiscretion, Mootie was reprimanding Bossie and making his feelings known about the matter.

I can remember asking Dog if they approached Mootie after they saw what was going on? Dog said that they certainly did not. He respected the rights of young lovers and felt that it was important for Mootie and Bossie to have quality private time together. This sensitivity of Dog's belied another one of his finer qualities, that of his belief in the power of true romance.

Another quality I truly respected about Dog was the pride he took in anyone he cared about. I say this because as I write I continually think of more and more things about Dog that I remember. He was a fine man but don't get me wrong - he had a side of him that loved fun, he was far from a choir boy, and if he was here he would tell you that. But he was a very decent man, a good man, and someone who'll be remembered by many of us for a long time to come. But the stories about him are just too good to let fade away....

Growing up in Juliette, as I mentioned earlier, afforded very few social outlets for young people. Church, school, and home were pretty much it. One thing my brother Ernest and I did a lot was shoot basketballs in our backyard. We were encouraged in this by Ed Jr. as he loved basketball and was even captain of the team at Mary Persons High. Anyway, Ernest and I played so much that we got to the point where we missed very few shots from certain spots on the court. We played tons of two-on-one games with my dad and learned that if we played with someone older than ourselves that the smart thing to do was to pass the ball around and let the old geezer tire himself out.

We got good enough at basketball that we beat different groups of guys that came by the house on occasion. One day Ernest and I were in the backyard shooting hoops. Ed Jr. was out front doing a little work on his cars. Suddenly we heard a truck coming up the dirt road that led into our driveway (the sound of the engine let us know if the vehicle approaching was a car or truck - we weren't right every time but were most of the time). As the truck came up the driveway we saw that it was Dog and Coogler. They had come by to talk chickens with Ed Jr. They parked their truck and got out, waved at Ernest and me, and began talking with my dad. Ernest and I kept on shooting hoops. During their discussion I kept noticing Ed Jr. motioning towards us. After a few more minutes of conversation my dad, Dog, and Coogler walked over to where we were shooting baskets.

We all shot the ball around for a few minutes. Ed Jr. was telling

Coogler and Dog how good Ernest and I were getting at playing basketball. After a few minutes of this, Dog looked up and said, "Tell you what - Coogler and I will play these two boys. And I'll bet we beat the hell out of them!" Ernest and I said OK and we all let Ed Jr. be the referee.

Ernest and I took the ball out and kept passing it back and forth between us. One of us would drive to the basket, turn, and pass the ball backwards to the other. Since we had played together so much over the years (this also helped us in baseball as Ernest played second base and I played shortstop - we turned a few double plays by just knowing how and where to feed the other the ball) we knew where the other would be on the court without even looking. The purpose of driving to the basket was twofold:

1) We might get an easy basket and/or;
2) We would run Dog and Coogler ragged.

This strategy paid off - if Ernest drove to the basket, he'd pass back to me and I'd make the outside shot. Then we would reverse the strategy so that I would drive and Ernest would shoot and we'd score again (and again and again). The game was relatively close at first. As it wore on, you could see Dog and Coogler starting to run out of gas. When we saw this, it made us press even harder. One thing you have to understand here is that the Williams family is extremely competitive. You play to win! You play fair and you understand that you may lose at times, but you play like hell to win. This philosophy extended from sports into board games into anything else that had a winner and loser involved. It is so ingrained in me that when I play games with my children I play to win! Debbie gets on to me about it but I actually think that they have to learn that this is a very competitive world. The sooner they learn this the better off they're going to be. One thing about it though, and I tell my kids this, is that a day will come when they'll start beating the pants off ole' dad in certain things. When that day occurs, no one will be prouder than I will be.

Back to the game - it went on and Dog and Coogler got more and more whipped out. Finally, with about a twenty to thirty point lead, the game was called. I can remember laughing because Dog and

Coogler were all bent over, red-faced, and gasping for air. When they got their breath, we all laughed and discussed the game. Ernest and I thought nothing more about it and went on about the rest of our day.

Ed Jr. told me later that Dog got the biggest kick out of telling his friends about that game - that he bragged to people about how good Ernest and I played. He also poked fun at his own performance (and Coogler's) and laughed hard about it. It was indicative of the type person he was - he played like hell to win but he also enjoyed the game and got great satisfaction that his nephews had outplayed him. It was hard not to like and respect someone who looked at things the way Dog did.

As I grew older and got involved in sports and dating and stuff, I didn't see Dog nearly as often as before. I would occasionally run into him in downtown Juliette or hear Ed Jr. mention him, but the contact we'd had slowed down considerably. When I went through college, got married, and proceeded to have a family, the communication between the two of us pretty much ground to a halt.

This makes me sad because I could've done something about it. Everytime Debbie and the kids and I would go to Juliette we would ride by Dog's house on highway 87. More than once I'd think about stopping in, but I was always too busy, or had work to do, or somewhere to go, or something else that kept me from visiting him. I remember a few years ago he dropped by my house one day to see us but we were all away somewhere. I probably hadn't seen Dog in five years or so at that point. After all those years and the poor effort on my part to see him, he still came by to visit me. He cared about my family and me. He was like that.

I guess it boils down to this - it's so easy to take life for granted. Those people closest to us appear to be invincible and we stupidly believe that they'll always be there. We can put off seeing them, or sending a card, or doing whatever else cause they'll always be around. This week, Debbie passed out in her car on I-75 while driving home. Fortunately, the airbags in the car saved her life - her car was absolutely totaled. Could I possibly have envisioned Debbie leaving one morning and never coming back? It is inconceivable - yet it nearly happened. How do you tell your children that their mother is dead? Think about it.....

I'll always miss Dog and think about him. And I'll think about how I let things like business and other nonessentials dissipate what was such a good relationship. I'll bet that right now somewhere up in heaven there's a group of guys sitting around a cockpit talkin'. A familiar laugh and southern drawl stands out among these voices - its Dog, and he's having a helluva good time. And I hope that if I'm up there with him some day that I'll have sense enough to be there watchin him pit 'em. May your soul rest well Dog.....

CHAPTER 16

CUPPIN' THE JEWELS

Let there be no doubt, Tommy Wilson should be the next President of the United States...

I don't say that lightly, either - I mean it. If I could somehow get Tommy on the ballot, I'd be casting my vote for him, and I'd be encouraging everyone else I know to do the same. Tommy's an ace, a man's man, and would make the best damn President this country has ever seen.

"Ed", you ask, "how can you say that? What qualifications does this man have that would make you give out that sort of endorsement? Please tell us just who in the hell this Tommy Wilson is?" That's reasonable - I'll do it, and then you'll understand why it will be a terrible injustice if Tommy Wilson isn't elected President of the United States one day...

Tommy is an old Monroe County boy, just like me. At the time I was growing up in Juliette, Tommy was growing up in High Falls. My parents worked hard, and barely made ends meet. Tommy's worked hard, and also barely made ends meet. We're both the same age, went to the same schools, and both of us loved sports. In fact, if the truth be known, both of us would have been tagged as being a tad "fanatical" about the things we loved doing. I craved listening to Elvis, smooching women, and singing rock 'n' roll music. Tommy craved fast cars, faster women, and politics. And both of us took our loves of these things and rolled them over into other aspects of our lives. So, any way you cut it, there are some pretty marked similarities between the two of us.

Tommy was great in school - he made nearly all "A's", and was very, very intelligent. But we also knew that he stayed up many nights studying, and that his grades didn't just happen by accident. Tommy was mentally gifted, but he fought hard for his grades, and you had to respect someone like that. He basically took his natural gifts, worked hard with them, and made himself even better during the process.

Another thing that drew attention to Tommy was the way he had with women. He wasn't one of those guys that was flashy about it, or talked about it a lot, but I guarantee you that Tommy knew lots of women. I'm not gonna come right out and speculate on why that was - it may have just been that Tommy was silky smooth in manner, or he may have been gifted in certain ways physically, or the attraction may have just been due to his winning personality. Whatever it was, Tommy had it in spades, because he was the only guy in school whose dates were assigned nicknames immediately after he took them out. Who could ever forget "Parentheses Legged Pam", or "California Heard", or "Moanin' Mary, With Bent Legs So Scary." None of them were known as such until Tommy spent some good quality alone time with them.

The thing, though, that impressed me most about Tommy was his athletic ability. He was a natural athlete, but, it was more than that that you noticed. Tommy worked like hell to be an even better athlete - he was the guy who stayed after football practice to run extra wind sprints, or the guy that stayed after the films of the game were shown to watch them all over again. I can remember racing against him in various types of running competitions. I would win some, he would win some, but I was always pushed, and he forced you to give him the best you had in the process. He was intense, focused, got results, and he made you do the same just to keep up with him. He was a true winner, pure and simple.

Now at this point you're probably saying, "Okay, so Tommy's a nice guy, he gives the women hell, but what about all that makes him a potentially great President? A lot of people have good qualities, but what sets him apart to that degree?"

It's still a fair question - let me explain it to you a bit more clearly, using one simple story from our past to make the needed points...

It's the fall of 1973, and the Mary Persons Bulldogs are playing the Manchester Blue Devils. This game is a huge deal each year, as Manchester and Mary Persons contended for sub-region and regional honors many, many times over the years. On account of that, a very intense rivalry was formed between the two schools. Manchester was always hard as hell to beat, and, when we did beat them, we were all proud of the accomplishment as they were such a first rate program. Their fans were committed and loyal, and their school was a damn good one. Manchester and Mary Persons became one of those true sports rivalries that we all remember, like Ali-Frazier, Palmer-Nicklaus, or The Rock-Triple H.

In 1973, our senior year, we found ourselves playing Manchester in Forsyth, a home game in front of a pack of screaming Mary Persons' fans. In this game, though, a rare thing happened - we gave Manchester a sure 'nuff, country asswhuppin'. Since that didn't hardly ever happen, you tend to remember it even more vividly now. Let's go back and pick this game up late in the third quarter, with the score being somewhere in the neighborhood of 34-7 (the final score ended at 41-7)...

Tommy and I happened to be in the game together on defense - I played safety, and Tommy was in at cornerback. In a game as one-sided as this one, your main objective on defense was not to let your opponent complete a long pass. Accordingly, Tommy and I are playing way back, willing to give up the short pass but not willing to give up a lengthy (and embarrassing as hell) bomb.

It's third down and about 15 to go for Manchester. They march up to the line, and their quarterback (who for some reason had a voice higher than a thirteen year old girl's with strep throat), squeaked off the signals, "Set, 22, hike, hike!"

On the snap, he fades back to pass, and Tommy and I fade back as well, ever alert to a long one. As Big Puddy and Whiff Walker (two of our stellar defensive linemen) closed in on Peter Pan, he dumps a pass off over the middle to their tight end. The tight end catches the ball, tucks it under, and begins making his way up field. Tommy and I immediately close in on him to make the tackle....

Tommy arrives at ground zero about one half step before I do, and we both knock the hell out of the guy. The only problem was, with Tommy getting there that half step sooner, he's in front of me, and, when the tackle commences, Tommy's right leg comes up and cracks me flush in the balls.

God, it hurt like nothing I'd ever felt in my life - I dropped right to my knees like a two dollar whore with an overdue rent payment. I was blinded, choking, and lying on the grass in a fetal position with both hands reverently squeezing my cardsack.

The pile of players in on the tackle eventually unstacked themselves, and Tommy and the tight end both got up. Not me - I was down on all fours, both hands holding a near death-like grip on my cardsack, with a queasy sort of feeling like the one I get when a religious book reviewer tells me they are going to be fair. I was hurtin', and hurtin' pretty damn badly.

Tommy does notice in a second or so that I'm not getting up, so he walks over to me to see just what the problem is. In his usual, concern filled voice, he says,

"Ed, you're holding your balls in front of the whole damn county."

As pain laden as I was, I was coherent enough to realize he was right - I was lyin' on the ground in the fetal position cuppin' the jewels in front of some six thousand or so people...

With this newfound knowledge, I struggled up, and, when I did I found that I could only stand with my hands on my knees - I couldn't stand fully upright due to the intensity of the pain. Pain or no pain, I did notice that Manchester was lining up for the next play.

As for me, I was ready to just lay down, give in to the pain, when Tommy looked over and yelled, "It's Manchester, goddammit - straighten up and get after 'em, you can hold your balls just as soon as we end this play!"

Pain or no pain, I was a Mary Persons Bulldog, and Tommy left no doubt with me that I was expected to play like one. I somehow shrugged off the pain and actually participated in the play. After that, I was replaced and went over to the sidelines, where a well placed ice bag slowly drained the pain off my wailing balls.

When the game ended, I went over and thanked Tommy for doing what he did. I couldn't help but respect the leadership skills that he had displayed. He looked at me and said, "I knew you had it in you, I knew you wouldn't lay down for those bastards even though your balls were hurting. Plus, to be honest, I was feelin' guilty as hell for kicking them, so gettin' you back up on your feet helped me to feel a whole lot better, too."

And there you have it - Tommy as he was, to the point, compassionate at times, but blunt as hell when he had to be. He was inspiring, coaxing, and always admonishing you to do your very best. The best thing about it all, though, was that he was only asking of you what he demanded of himself each day of his life.

When you sum it all up, what does it all tell you? Well, it tells you exactly what qualities you try to find in a leader, a potential President of the United States. You want someone resourceful, kind, yet forceful when he needs to be. A man who can tenderly kiss America's ass one minute, then, give us a good, swift kick to the balls the next when we need it. A man who knows the right time to dispense either tough or tender love. Bottom line, a man a whole lot like Tommy Wilson....

Think about all this the next time a national election comes up. It wouldn't take a whole lot to get Tommy's name on some state ballots and then let a little momentum build. Before we'd all know it, Tommy would be driving up Pennsylvania Avenue and straight on into the White House. And I promise ya'll, if he becomes President and ever lets any of us down, I'll go personally up to the White House myself and kick his balls at just the right moment, preferably when he's addressing a national television audience so that we can all get the full enjoyment out of it. Besides, once Tommy gets over the pain he'll ultimately appreciate what I did for him, thank me for it, and, even if he doesn't, he knows that I still owe him one anyway....

CHAPTER 17

MUMP SHOTS,
AND BARIUM ENEMAS

I know that just by this title that many of ya'll will find this chapter to be particularly appetizing - mump shots and barium enemas. Scrumptious sounding isn't it? There's actually some logic here, as you will see as you read further....

I got to thinking about mump shots and barium enemas right after Debbie's car accident. Fortunately, as I told you, she was okay but did get bruised up pretty good. She had to spend one night in the hospital so that the staff could generally observe her and make sure that she was okay. Anyway, Debbie mentioned while in the hospital that she had had to get a few more shots and drink a load of barium so that the doctors could more thoroughly check her out. When she told me that, I burst out laughing! Since this was a pretty unusual reaction given the situation, Debbie demanded to know what I was laughing about. Well, this is where I found the humour................

Back when I was about ten or eleven years old my brother Ernest came down with a case of the mumps. You really couldn't tell it cause all it did was make his neck swell up a little and cause a low grade fever. When this didn't go away after a couple of days my mom took him to see Dr. Bramblett. Dr. Bramblett examined my brother and quickly told my mother that he had a case of the mumps. We came home after that, made my brother as comfortable as possible, and continued on with the day's routine.

Ed Jr. worked the day shift that day and got home around four o'clock. When he walked in the door I said, "Dad, we know what's wrong with Big Dolphin!" (Big Dolphin was the nickname that my brother Ernest got tagged with. I really don't remember where this nickname came from except that my brother is big. Where the Dolphin part came from I haven't a clue). Anyway, my dad sort of looked up and asked what it was. I told him, "The mumps - Dr. Bramblett said he's had 'em for three or four days now!"

The color sort of drained from Ed Jr.'s face. "You mean——the damn mumps?" he asked. "Yes the mumps", I replied. Ed Jr. then hollered out for my mom.

She came into the room and asked him what the problem was. "I'll tell you what the damn problem is," Ed Jr. exclaimed, "the problem is that the Dolphin has the mumps and I've never had them!" My mom said okay but asked him why he was so upset about it? "Barbara, I'll tell you why I'm upset - the mumps can make it where you'll never be able to have children again!" he shouted. My mom smiled and said, "I didn't think you wanted anymore children anyway." Ed Jr. then yelled out, "I don't want anymore but I sure as hell want to be able to make some if I change my mind!"

You can't question that logic. Anyway, Ed Jr. went on and on about the situation for awhile when my mother said, "You know, there are mumps vaccines. If you really are serious about not wanting to get the mumps, you can go to Forsyth and let Dr. Bramblett give you a mumps shot."

Our kitchen got very quiet (for some reason, all major Williams family discussions were held in the kitchen) as it was well known in our house that my dad was not fond of shots. It was amusing watching his facial expressions after my mom made the suggestion - Ed Jr. looked as serious as a pitcher trying to get an out when the bases are loaded. He thought about the suggestion for what seemed like hours and finally said, "I'm gettin the damn shot. You better come with me Al, and get one too."

All the humour that I had worked up over the situation sort of vanished. Actually not sort of - it evaporated like a keg of beer at a frat party. Anyway, there was no choice. My dad did not operate our house using democratic principles - I was going to have to get the shot, no two ways about it.

We got in our old blue Ford Falcon (1965) the next morning to make our trek to Forsyth. You would have thought that we were two attendees at a funeral (or the guests of honor) from the silence that engulfed the car during the ride. I can't say for sure what Ed Jr. was thinking about but I was doing my usual psyche job over getting a shot. Normally, when I was about to receive a shot, it took me some time to get into the mental state necessary to endure it. I hate a damn shot - still do today, in fact. I think though that my fear of shots stemmed from my early days with Dr. Bramblett. Don't get me wrong - Dr. Bramblett was a great doctor and our family loved him. The only thing bad about getting a shot at Dr. Bramblett's office was that his nurse Ruth gave it to you. Ruth was a great person as well - kind, considerate, and she took good care of our family. The problem with Ruth was the way she gave you shots. Ruth, when giving a shot, would hold your arm with one hand firmly. Then, she would position the syringe in the other hand like a javelin thrower about to toss the javelin. Without any warning she would plunge the needle into your arm. It hurt like hell and the anticipation beforehand made it even worse. I would rather have dressed up in my Sunday best two hundred times than have to get a shot from Ruth.

The Falcon got us to Forsyth and soon Ed Jr. and I arrived at Dr. Bramblett's office. We got out of the car, walked into Dr. Bramblett's office, and waited for our appointments with that hot needle.

Apparently the mumps were making the rounds cause we had to wait a good while. Once during the wait I looked over at Ed Jr. He looked like he would rather have kissed a cow's ass than go through with these shots. I thought about our situation, and decided I would ask Ed Jr. if we could just go. Neither one of us wanted to be there - let's just leave and go home. Mom wouldn't even have to know.

I mentioned this idea to Ed Jr. - he paused, thought it over, looked at me and said, "Son, if we don't get these shots our balls will swell up bigger than hams." I wasn't very old but I knew enough to know that I didn't my balls to be mistaken for hams. The die was firmly cast and I knew that the shots were coming.

After what seemed to be an eternity, the receptionist for Dr.

Bramblett told us that he was ready to see us. Ed Jr. and I trudged into Dr. Bramblett's office. When we got there, Dr. Bramblett told us that Ruth was out sick and that he would be administering the shots. For me, this was great news and definitely made me feel better about the whole situation. For Ed Jr., the announcement didn't seem to make a whole lot of difference. He had the same grim look on his face that he'd had since we had gotten into the car to make the trip.

Dr. Bramblett walked over and pulled out a normal-sized syringe to give me my mumps shot (its funny - one thing I've always noticed about myself is whenever I am supposed to get a shot my legs hurt. I know that has no relevance to this story but I thought I'd throw it in). He went over and stuck the needle into a container of mumps vaccine. He drew out a relatively small amount and walked over to me.

You know, the worst part about a shot is when they spread that alcohol on your arm before they jab it to you. You feel the cool alcohol and the cotton ball on your arm and you know that the impalation is about to occur. I stood there, awaiting my injury from Dr. Bramblett.

I felt a slight sting - the needle was in my arm! To Dr. Bramblett's credit it hurt hardly any. Before I knew it, he pulled the needle out and told me he was done. He dabbed a little more alcohol on my arm, told me to roll my sleeve down, and to wait over in the corner for my dad. I did exactly as asked and walked over and stood in a corner of the room.

The reason I stood in a corner was that it was now time for the main event - Ed Jr.'s turn to take the needle. My dad had been quite reassuring when I was getting my shot but he was ghostly quiet now. He looked sort of pale and gave off a demeanor that suggested that he would rather get a tooth pulled without anesthetic than to undergo the shot. Dr. Bramblett and Ed Jr. talked for a few minutes and then Dr. Bramblett went over to get a syringe to plunk in the old man's arm.

I noticed with interest that Dr. Bramblett did not go over to the box that he got my syringe from - he went over to another box. He pulled out a syringe that I swear to God was big enough to inoculate a horse! It was huge - probably three times bigger than the one I got nailed with. Dr. Bramblett pulled it out of the box and held it up. Ed Jr. looked at this syringe like someone had just announced that the plane he was flying in had lost its engines or something. He stammered out, "Goddamn, Doc! You ain't gonna give me a shot with that are you? That looks like something you would inoculate a farm animal with!"

Dr. Bramblett very calmly stated, "Ed, mumps vaccine is given in amounts relative to the size of the person being inoculated. Your son only weighs eighty-five pounds, therefore, he got a small amount of the vaccine. On the other hand you weigh two hundred and twenty pounds so you must take a larger amount of the medicine. Now Ed, we both know you don't want the mumps."

At this point, it wouldn't have surprised me if Ed Jr. had declared that he would take his chances with the mumps. I guess though that with me and Dr. Bramblett standing there that there was no way that he could weenie out. He would bravely undergo his shot. As he told me years later, "...a man that can survive the Korean War can damn well take a shot. But it was a damn big shot........"

The next surprise for my dad came when Dr. Bramblett told him to drop his britches. Ed Jr. looked funny and blurted out, "You mean I gotta take it in the ass, Doc?" Dr. Bramblett replied that with the large amount of mumps vaccine that he was being given that the shot needed to be given in a fleshy part of the body so that the medicine would disperse easily. Dr. Bramblett added that since I was so light it really didn't matter whether I got mine in the arm or "buttocks." The pending ass shot didn't really help Ed Jr.'s demeanor, but Dr. Bramblett had other patients to see and needed to get through with us.

Dr. Bramblett put the syringe into the mumps vaccine. I swear it looked like he pulled half a quart of it into the syringe. Once he had done this, he told Ed Jr. to drop his britches and bend over. I immediately had to stifle the impulse to laugh out loud.

Here was Ed Jr. - nervous as hell about this shot - dropping his pants in Dr. Bramblett's office. He bent over the table and I thought I was going to lose it. I dared not laugh out loud as my dad would've gone through the roof, but, how could I keep from laughing? Here was Ed Jr., bent over the table at Dr. Bramblett's office, his fat old hairy ass sticking out, and Dr. Bramblett getting ready to inoculate him with a needle that looks like it should've been used on a rogue elephant. Dr. Bramblett eased the needle into those big cheeks and began to push the serum in. Because of the half-quart or so he had to inject it was a very slow process. Ed Jr.'s ass cheeks tensed up and quivered several times. It was so funny that my eyes got teary - the only reason that I kept from laughing out loud was I developed this fear that if I laughed that Ed Jr. would have Dr. Bramblett vaccinate me for the Asian measles or something. This would mean another shot and I definitely didn't want that.

Dr. Bramblett finally finished with my dad's shot. Ed Jr. then stood up and got his britches up as fast as I've ever seen anyone do it. As soon as that task was complete, we were in the Falcon and on our way home.

Ed Jr. had a serious, pensive (Foskey-type) look going the whole way home. A couple of times he complained that his ass hurt from the shot. I kidded him and told him that I thought the needle looked like a harpoon or something. He was already on the mend enough at this point to laugh at the comment. We drove on and soon pulled into the driveway. As he got out, Ed Jr. looked at me and said something that ought to be inscribed and recorded for posterity, "You know, son, that damn shot was good for us. We needed it and it was the best thing to do. But, like a lot of other things that are supposed to be good for us, it was a pain in the ass!" With this, Ed Jr. was satisfied, the mumps issue was closed, and we went on about our daily lives.

Let's get back to the conversation Debbie and I were having at the hospital. I tracked her through the mumps shot episode that I just related. We both laughed and then I got quiet. I thought a few minutes and then couldn't help but laugh again. Debbie looked at me and said that she questioned my sanity sometimes. I agreed with her that it should be questioned but I still couldn't stop laughing. I told her that it was her fault for bringing the subject of barium enemas up in the first place. She asked what was so funny about barium enemas and I replied that it just so happened that Ed Jr. had received a barium enema. Debbie said, "I know I'm going to regret having asked this but what happened?" I smiled and began the story..........

It seems that about fifteen or twenty years ago Ed Jr. was having some digestive tract problems of some sort. To tell you the truth, I really can't remember what was causing the difficulties. Whatever it was, his doctor told him that he had to have a barium enema. You would have thought that he was going to have open heart surgery or something from the way he complained about it.

Ed Jr. went to work and related the fact that he was going to have to have a barium enema. One of his friends at work, Barlow, told my dad of his barium enema experiences. Apparently Barlow had to have one of these things done. He went to see his doctor and the doctor told Barlow that a barium enema would have to be administered. Barlow, being a red-blooded American male, wanted to have this done about as much as he wanted to convert to socialism. The doctor insisted that the procedure had to be done as some x-rays of Barlow's internal organs needed to be taken to ensure that his health was not at risk. With tons of reservations about the entire process, Barlow bent over and awaited his fate......

Apparently, barium has to be (how do I say this delicately) pumped into a person. This is what the doctor proceeded to do with Barlow. He pumped barium into him through the enema. Barlow recalled that it hurt like hell and that he kept asking the doctor as to when was he gonna stop? The doctor told Barlow at first to hold it down, that there was plenty of room for the barium he was injecting. Barlow gritted his teeth and went along with this at first. The minutes went by and more and more barium was injected. Barlow was starting to feel severe pressure in his lower abdominal region. Barlow then looked at the doc and told him that he was pretty full of barium. He then admonished the doctor not to give him any more. The doctor said that there was still more to be pumped in and that Barlow should just be quiet and make the best of the experience. Barlow said that that was a crock of crap, that he couldn't take anymore. The doctor somehow managed to quiet him down and kept pumping the barium to him. In a few more minutes Barlow, with a red-tinted face, implored the doctor to immediately stop pumping the barium. The doctor told him yet again that he was exaggerating. Barlow told him that he was serious and that he was "at capacity." The doc wouldn't stop pumping the stuff. Barlow finally hollered out, "Stop this dammit, I'm full!" The doc still wouldn't listen. At this point, Barlow's rectum expelled the enema knozzle like a missile and he proceeded to coat the walls, floor, and equipment in the lab with barium! Barlow said it took him about half a minute to cover the place. He then turned, looked at the doctor, and said, "Just how damn smart are you? Does a man have to tell you twenty times that his ass is full of barium?" The doc admitted that he made an error in judgment and they proceeded from there....

Ed Jr. related this tender experience to us at the dinner table one night. You can imagine that Brother and I laughed until we turned red and our stomachs hurt. Mama, on the other hand, was not amused and told my dad that he had the tact and manners of Godzilla.

A couple of weeks went by and it was close to time for Ed Jr.'s enema. You would've thought that my dad was about to captain a crew on the space shuttle or something from the way he went on about it. He talked about the time he had to be there (10 am), what his doctor had told him (same doctor that Barlow had - apparently Ed Jr. felt that after Barlow's experience that this particular doctor would damn well listen when he was told that the patient was "at capacity"), and how he couldn't eat for twenty-four hours prior to the enema. The only good thing about all this was that our whole family felt that we were well versed in the vagaries of the barium enema process. Anyway, before we knew it, the night before the enema ("Enema Eve") arrived.

You have to understand that the one firm tradition we had in the Williams' family household was that we ate well - very well. My dad had a huge appetite, my brother a good one, and I, even though physically the smallest of the three, had the biggest appetite in the whole bunch (for the record, at that time, my dad was six feet, one inches tall and weighed about two hundred twenty pounds; my brother was six feet, three inches tall and weighed about two hundred thirty-five pounds; and I was five feet, nine inches tall and weighed about one hundred forty-five pounds). It was common for all three of us to eat a huge dinner and then have milk shakes afterwards, typically around nine PM. Now when I say milkshakes I mean milkshakes! Ed Jr. bought these three huge plastic glasses - they looked like they would hold half a gallon of liquid in them. They were made of very thick, solid plastic - you couldn't have broken one of these glasses if it was dropped over the side of Niagara Falls. Anyway, about nine PM each evening Ed Jr. would look over at Brother and I whilst watching TV and say, "Want a shake?" We always replied that we did.

Ed Jr. would then go in the kitchen and pull out these three plastic tumblers (as he called them). He would take out a one-half gallon container of vanilla ice cream (my mom bought a half-gallon of it each day) and split it up between the three glasses. Then, he would pull out a half-gallon of chocolate milk (also purchased every day) and cover the ice cream with the milk. Believe you me, when he put the ice cream in the glasses he really packed it down - you ended up with a huge shake when he finished making these things. He would concoct these milkshakes and then bring them into the den for the three of us. It's a wonder we all didn't all weigh about four hundred pounds each with the kind of diets we maintained.

So it was that each night we had a huge meal and a milkshake. And now, on Enema Eve, my dad could not have anything to eat. This bothered Ed Jr. so much that he called the doctor at home that evening to be sure that the milkshake couldn't be consumed ("...after all doc, it's not solid food..."). When he found out that water was all he could have, he cussed about the sacrifices modern medicine had imposed on him for the remainder of the evening.

Bright and early the next morning Ed Jr. made the trek to Macon for his enema. He was none too happy as he left for his appointment. As was typically the case with him, he bemoaned his fate pretty loudly but knew inherently that he had to do it. "Going to a doctor is like getting a phone call, son - most times its not a good experience", he stated before going off to Macon. He gamely got into the old '65 Falcon and sped away.

My dad said that he arrived at the doctor's office early and had to wait around as the doctor was tied up. After about a thirty-to-forty minute wait Ed Jr. was ushered into his office. He had his blood pressure checked, answered some routine questions, and was told to go into a dressing room and change into a hospital gown. I would've given fifty dollars to have seen my old man in a hospital gown. With his hairy legs and ass, his stocky build, and his general demeanor about the whole situation, I'm sure I would've rolled in the floor laughing at the gowned Ed Jr. He came out and was escorted into another room.

Ed Jr. knew from Barlow's description that this was the room the enema would be administered in. He looked around and noted the single lab table, the enema equipment, and all the other miracles that modern medicine had wrought over the years. To say Ed Jr. was feeling queasy would've been an understatement, but, he had no choice but to somehow get through the impending misery and then he could return home.

The doctor walked in and right off the bat Ed Jr. advised him that he knew him because his friend Barlow had just had this same procedure performed a short while ago. Ed Jr. looked the doc right in the eye and said, "Doc, when I tell you I've had enough, I mean it. Okay?" The doctor instantly comprehended what he was being asked, agreed, and went on getting prepared for the big event.

Ed Jr. said that only once during the experience did he have to tell the doctor that he had had enough barium. He said that the doctor asked him if he felt full? Ed Jr. replied that if he got any fuller the doctor's office would be the scene of the second Hindenburg disaster. The doc got Ed Jr.'s message and lightened up.

My dad got up when it was all over and was told to step into a private restroom area for patients who had just had the barium enema procedure performed. Ed Jr. walked in and said the place was nothing but stalls. He staggered over, sat down, and shut the door in one of them.

A few minutes went by and Ed Jr. noticed a woman entering this bathroom. He said he could see her through a crack in the door (apparently this bathroom was a unisex facility). He instantly noticed that she was very overweight, scaling in at around three hundred plus pounds. She also was moaning loudly. This upset Ed Jr because, as he put it, "We all know it hurt like hell but why make an issue out of it?" He said that she walked very slowly, holding her rear end and moaning stuff like, "Oh God in heaven", "help me Jesus", "my damn ass is killing me", and other such quaint sayings. Of the more than several stalls in the facility, Miss Cellulite picks out one right next to my dad.

Ed Jr. was suffering enough as it was but he said that this woman just wouldn't shut up. She was moaning out to God and stuff and just spreading misery well over into Ed Jr.'s stall. My dad said that what made it all the worse was that as you expelled the barium you farted a lot. Being the southern gentleman that he is, Ed Jr. felt badly about breaking wind with a lady close by. But, as is sometimes the case, nature overtook manners and Ed Jr. unleashed a barium tuba concerto in his stall.

Miss Cellulite cleared her throat and haughtily told Ed Jr. that he was making disgusting sounds and that he must stop immediately. My dad said that this made him so mad that he bore down and ripped off another barrage just to show his displeasure. After this noxious display she threatened to go tell the doctors that she was being annoyed. Ed Jr. got upset and said, "Look, we just had a damn barium enema. We have got to get this crap out of our systems. Now I can't help that, but you could have taken your fat ass down to the other end and sat in one of those stalls. Nobody asked you to sit next to me - now get a damn life and shut your mouth!" This woman said that she had never been talked to like that before in her life. Ed Jr. stated that if someone had talked more firmly with her before that she wouldn't be the fat, wheezing slug that she was now. With that retort, Ed Jr. stated that their relationship pretty much fizzled out.......

My dad finished his business, got up, and walked out to get his clothes. The nurse in charge of the barium department walked up to him and asked how he felt? My dad said that he looked at her incredulously and asked where his clothes were? She told him where they were and also said that the doctor might have a few more questions to ask him. Would he mind waiting? Ed Jr. stated that the doctor had his phone number and that he was free to call him anytime he wanted. With that, he got his clothes and got dressed. Then, he very quickly got into our '65 blue Ford Falcon and drove home.

Debbie of course was more primed than ever to go through her situation after hearing this tender tale. After I related this episode, she looked at me and said, "Did ya'll ever do anything in the Williams' family that wasn't an unusual experience?"

Gosh, I don't really think so........

CHAPTER 18

THE COLUMNS

You know, since all this writing and book stuff started, I've had several people suggest to me that I should start writing columns. After getting some instruction from a column writing friend of mine, I proceeded to knock off five of these short epistles, just to see if I could do it. The amazing thing is that I already have a couple of newspapers asking about them, which goes to show you the incredible lack of judgment these days in the newspaper business.

This is the one chapter "PG-rated" enough that you can let the teenager who's been bugging the hell out of you about reading this book (but you haven't let them, cause you were afraid they might think you did some of the same stuff I did when you were growing up), read...

Civic Beautification

Sometimes, I think we really need to re-examine our logic...

A while back I was riding into downtown Macon with my company's insurance broker, Charlie Deaton. We were heading there to go to the old Green Jacket Restaurant for a tad of lunch.

While on our trip to the Green Jacket, we passed the newly built Georgia Music Hall of Fame, and then, the Georgia Sports Hall of Fame.

I couldn't help notice as we rode by these buildings just how beautiful they are. They're both state-of-the-art structures, and aesthetically quite pleasing. They have it all - landscaped grounds, multiple sculptures, and wonderful ornamental fixtures.

One other thing they had was an old bum walking right past them....

This wasn't just any bum. This was a haint ugly bum. His gut was so large it really needed a wheelbarrow to support it. His face appeared to have been unshaven for days, and his countenance rivaled that of a very angered badger. He was, as Ed Jr. terms it, "triple-haint ugly."

And there he was walking right in front of these incredibly perfect buildings... The thought hit me immediately - why were we taxpayers allowing this? Why would we spend millions of dollars on beautiful buildings, just to allow one Charlie Pound look-alike to ruin their beauty? Is this what all our tax money was being spent for, to provide this ghastly contrast?

There is an easier way. Charlie and I thought it up as we were making our second trip back to the salad bar. Its profound, yet simple, which should mean it'll have some chance for wide appeal and acceptance. Just consider this idea...

We all know that when people go to renew their driver's licenses, they have to stand in front of one of those little mounted cameras to get their pictures taken. It would be an easy thing to hook up a computer to this camera that has an image of a decent looking person scanned into it. This person could be a level "six" on an ugly to beauty scale of one to ten. When the camera is activated, it could scan the face of the person being photographed, and give them an objective numeric rating based on the afore-mentioned scale.

A six could be the passing score - this would allow the person to walk out into public just as they are. Less than six? Why, a government issued mask (maybe like those the pro wrestlers wear) could be issued to the offendee. We could insure that the mask itself would lend itself to the beautification of the area the guilty party spends lots of time in. For example, green tinted masks could be issued for country residents (to blend in with the scenery) and concrete or asphalt colored masks could be employed by city dwellers.

This concept would not only improve city and country beautification, but could also cause a whole series of cottage industry spin-offs. Imagine apartment communities for those with scores of one to three (no lights needed there), or guard services for those with scores of eight or greater. Human scarecrows could suddenly come into vogue. Bottom line, it doesn't take a genius to see that this thing could be an incredible boon for business. And if business does well, the tax dollars collected goes up, and then more government sponsored services could be rendered to all citizens. I have to modestly say that this is an incredible idea, it could even go worldwide, and ya'll can thank Charlie and I for it if you happen run into us one day. Wonder why the mayor isn't returning my calls these days?

Burr Ball

The other night as I was watching a Braves' game, the announcers started droning on and on about how much skill it took to play baseball. They got into the speed and types of pitches, conditioning and reflexes, split second decision making, all sorts of stuff like that. You can just about imagine the dialogue as we've heard it all about a million times before.

Well, they can talk pro baseball all they want to in terms of skill, but it runs a far distant second to a real man's sport - its cousin and derivative, "burr ball."

For the few of you out there who don't know what burr ball is, its a game we played in my backyard in Juliette when I was growing up. Ed Jr. was the originator, and no game I've ever played, before or since, has proved as challenging as burr ball.

For burr ball, you played a one-on-one match-up. There was a hitter and pitcher, and that was it. An axe handle served as the bat, and the hitter was stationed about twenty-five feet behind our house in the backyard, and was pointed at the house. The rules were simple - each side had three outs, the games were nine innings, if you hit one over the roof it was a home run, if you hit one on the roof it was an out if the pitcher caught it before it touched the ground. If he dropped it, you had a hit and a runner on base.

Hitting wasn't what made burr ball challenging, though - it was the pitching, and what was pitched, that accomplished that. What was pitched was one of three items:

>Dried up sweet gum burrs that were placed in a pail of water.
>Dried up hickory nut shell quarters.
>Full, green hickory nuts.

Think hitting those items wasn't a challenge? That was only the half of it, cause the man that pitched them to me, Ed Jr., was the recognized Greg Maddux of burr ball.

Let me give you an idea - it would be my turn at bat, and I'd be holding that axe handle, standing about twenty feet from Ed Jr. He'd have a grimace on his face, and would stare at me for the longest period of time. In his right hand he held what might be a burr, a hickory nut, or a hickory nut shell. You never knew which one he would use, although you did know that he at least had a burr in his hand cause of the water that would be dripping off his fist.

He would go into the windup, and let it fly. If it was a burr, it'd come streaking in fast with water flying off it. It was so tiny it was hard to see, and the bad thing was, even if you hit it, it was typically a weak grounder that didn't even get up on the roof. If he threw the hickory nut, you'd never see it at all - you'd just swing and hope for contact, although that hardly ever happened. Ed Jr. would continually feed you burrs and hickory nuts until he knew you were his.

When that point came, when he knew you were looking burr or hickory, he'd sail up a dry hickory nut shell to the plate, the "flutterball". It would float in like a butterfly and land right at your feet. It was so slow coming up that you'd swing five or six times before it ever reached the plate and you'd never hit it. Ed Jr. always liked to get strike three on me with the "flutterball". He was so sure of it that he would even tell me when he was about to throw one, and, even then, I'd never hit it.

Ed Jr. never lost at burr ball, and I can never remember getting more than two hits off him in any single game. So just remember, when you hear Skip, Don, or any of those guys talking skill, just understand that they are pushing a very over-hyped sport. The number two athletically demanding sport, at best. You don't believe that? Well, just handpick a few Braves' players, invite 'em over to Juliette, give 'em an axe handle, and put 'em out there with Ed Jr. - the issue will quickly be put to rest then...

Exploding Whales

Its amazing what a little father-son television can turn up on a Tuesday night. Just last week, Will summoned me into the den to watch something called, "The World's Most Bizarre Home Videos."

They sure had the title pegged right. We saw all sorts of weird segments, but, one part of the program reaffirmed certain aspects about both politics and life to me...

It seems that recently on a beach out in California the high tides brought in a whale and deposited it. It was a dead whale, and I'm sure just sort of rolled up on the beach like...well...a dead whale would.

Well, as nature intends, tides do go back out, and this erstwhile Shamu was left behind lying on the sand. And out in the hot sun. And starting to be the focus of attack for a large variety of flies, buzzards, and other assorted natural scavengers.

Fortunately, for the residents of this beachfront community, city government was notified about the problem, and two members of the town's council promptly showed up at the beach to resolve it.

It couldn't have been pretty - kids swarming around the carcass, the odor of sulfur times ten in the air.

Fortunately, these town council members were out there on that razor's edge when it comes to creative thinking..

They decided to explode the whale - I mean it - literally explode the whale. As they explained it, "We figure some explosive charges placed under the whale, angled properly, will explode the carcass and deposit the chunks out into the ocean, where they will be naturally disposed of." You can't dispute that sound logic. Of course, the Titanic made sense, too. And, in this case, as in so many others, human error reared its ugly head...

Demolition experts came out, and put all sorts of explosive charges underneath the whale. They measured and talked and measured yet again. I did notice during all this activity that one of the demolition guys was actually chomping on a sandwich while standing about ten feet from this aromatic carcass. Now there's a man I'd love to invite to one of my mother-in-laws' social gatherings...

Finally, all the calculations were completed, and the explosives set in place underneath Moby Dick's fragrant body. The word was given, and the explosions began....

It was wild - a cloud of pink immediately consumed the air around the whale. Chunks of Shamu were flying about everywhere.

The only problem was that the demolition experts miscalculated in their judgments as to how much explosive power was needed to dispose of the corpse. Instead of blowing those sweet chunks out to sea, they exploded out in the opposite direction - landing, like stinky missiles, all over the beach itself.

You couldn't help but laugh - festering whale blubber chunks plopping around all over the beach. The video camera caught people ducking the chunks, and one roughly two hundred pound missile was filmed destroying a brand new Ford Mustang convertible. One fellow, covered in pink from head to toe, made the following astute observation...

"Its not the blood and guts that bother you, its the stench."

And there you have it - a major life's lesson learned. Will did ask me how those demolition experts could have screwed up so badly? I told him the sandwich eating guy probably made the calculations, and that, at worst, knew that a mistake would end up landing him and his town on "The World's Most Bizarre Home Videos." Probably figured the exposure would also help the town's tourism business.

Will nodded at my answer, and once again we both were left feeling incredibly awed by the remarkable efficiency of government, and the educational value of network TV...

Men, Women, and Toilet Paper Rolls...

At work several days ago, I walked into the kitchen area of our office early one morning to grab a large cup of coffee. Having slept nada the night before due to my typically horrible nocturnal habits, I desperately needed some chemical means of survival for the upcoming day. While walking in to grab some that I secretly hoped was stronger than a five day old Nu-Way hot dog, I heard Ray and Bob, two of our carpenters, make the following comment to Lynn, who works in purchasing....

"I always put the toilet paper on the holder however I pull it out of the bag." Made perfect sense to me. I even wondered why the topic was being discussed at all. Funny thing was, Ray's remark didn't seem to make any sense at all to Lynn. She replied back, "How could you be that insensitive? Any man that cares about his woman knows that you always put the roll in the holder so that the paper unfolds from the top. It's unladylike to have to scramble around and reach underneath the roll. What if someone accidentally walked in on you while you were doing that and saw you? It's too horrible to even imagine."

Ray, as polite a man as you'll ever see, apologized profusely for his terrible lack of toilet paper etiquette, and then got out of the office as quickly as he could. I didn't blame him, either. After a second or so of incredibly concentrated thought, I decided to pursue the toilet paper issue with Lynn just a little bit further....

"Lynn, wouldn't it be easier to just slip your hand underneath the roll? Seems to me that would be less strain on your hand and all."

Lynn glared at me like I'd just proposed that we kill her cat with toothpicks. She replied, "Ed, this may come as a surprise, but women are built differently than men. Its not as easy for us to reach under the toilet paper roll as it is for you."

I feigned shock at this, even though my own personal research into the "women are built differently than men" issue have proven her comments true many, many times before. Not to worry, though. I figured I'd mount the offensive again by saying, "Lynn, I really can't believe that this would be an issue at all between men and women." I was proud of this strategy, and said the words just a tad haughtily, so she'd see that this whole topic was crazy and beneath her.

"Ed, if you're that ignorant of such basic genetic and scientific fact, I guess I won't ever be able to convince you. But do yourself a favor - don't give your viewpoints on this to any women's organizations or clubs when you're out there making speeches. Its okay that you and I know that you're clueless about this issue, but, no need for you to spread the word around to the general population. It can be our little secret."

Know the bad thing? That got me to believing her viewpoint, so much so that when I walked in my house that evening, I did a quick quality control check on the positioning of all the toilet paper rolls in our bathrooms. I did flip a couple of them around, and thought I was being pretty discreet, but that ended when my wife walked in on me in flipping the third (and last one) over in our downstairs bathroom, "What're you doing?"

"I was just thinking about you, and decided to make sure that the toilet paper is in the right position on all the rolls for you."

She smiled and replied, "That's great, angel, but everyone knows that you put it on the roll where you can unfold it from the bottom. It's easier for a lady to pull some off that way. Women are a little bit different from men, you know."

And there you have it. They sure are. All that I could do at that point was to mosey on out into the backyard, slip into my hammock, and reflect on how much simpler the usage of the old corncob was.....

Capital Punishment

I know that writing a column about capital punishment is a no-win proposition. It's a sensitive issue, people's opinions are all over the map, so its something only a fool would discuss. That's the bottom line. Any logical, thinking person would scramble away from the topic as fast as they could. I'm fully aware of all that, you know.

Well, screw logic and thinking. I want to talk a tad about capital punishment, and I'm going to. Its the writer's privilege, to discuss whatever strikes their inner artistic chords. I promise I won't get all in-depth about the pros and cons or whatever, but since it is the law here in Georgia, its a ripe topic for discussion. And I want to discuss it, from a couple of vantage points.

The first point meriting discussion is how can someone condemned approach it all so calmly? Most accounts I've read suggest that the prisoners treat it as if all the upcoming festivities are little more than a casual Sunday stroll in the park. They receive visitors, take phone calls, and make the whole thing into a pretty folksy little interlude.....

Well, not me. I wouldn't go down that easy. I'd be wanting to drink massive quantities of liquor, experiment with drugs, and do anything else that would put me totally out of it. I'd yell and rant like a crazy man, sing Elvis medleys, and do anything that might convince those around me that I was insane, and worthy of sentence commutation. Paint my heiny pink and dance the watusi? I'd do it. Eat the paint off the wall? Hand me a spoon. If I'm not going for broke in this situation, I'm never going for broke. Just tell me what I need to do to get my about-to-be parched heiny off the hook.

The other point meriting discussion is what happens to you after you die in the chair. Now, there are all sorts of theological interpretations regarding life after death, and what all that amounts to. And all of that segues into heaven and hell, and what to expect if you find yourself in either place. I don't want to discuss heaven, as I think everyone is in general agreement that its a pretty good deal. What I wonder is what is hell like? I think the worst imaginable hell for me would be for ole'Satan, right after my newcomer orientation, to walk me into a room with a table and chair in front of it. On this table would be a record player, and yes, I do mean a record player. None of this modern CD ROM crap for me, I'd want to get back to basics, and basics for me is vinyl. Satan would tell me to sit down, and of course, since he's the devil and runs the show in hell, I'd have to do it. Then, I would be glued into the chair and two large stacks of albums would be placed before me. One stack would have a pile of Elvis and BTO albums in it. The only problem would be that they are all just beyond my reach. The second stack, easily reachable, would be a whole bunch of

Perry Como albums. And that, folks, would be my concept of pure hell, having to spend eternity listening to Perry while Elvis and BTO were just out of reach. I can't imagine anything worse, unless it involved being able to eat nothing but beets forever, and that thought is so horrible I won't even allow my brain to mull it out.

With all that said, you can see that I'll never make the trip to death row. I'm staying right here, and practicing sins that are more fun and less risky. The chair I could take, but an eternity of Perry? No way....

ABOUT THE AUTHOR

By Kelly Milner Halls

Most "About the Author" prefaces talk about the writer's kindergarten beginnings - reflections on literary prowess and proclivities beyond those of any normal child. But my relationship with Ed didn't begin in elementary school in Juliette, Georgia. My relationship with Ed started online.

We were both in our late thirties when this adventure took root. He was known as Balboa on Internet Relay Chat (IRC). I was code-named DinoLvr, after a book I'd written (sold and seen published) on dinosaurs.

It was virtual kismet that we "met." Rumor was I had cyber-romanced every other man on the 'Net. And Ed's Balboa persona had supposedly cyber-seduced half the women of #writers - the chat channel for scribes with more time than inspiration on their hands.

With a Romeo rep like that, it didn't surprise me to find he'd written a book called, "Sex, Dead Dogs, and Me: The Juliette Journals." What did surprise me was the fact that it was good. Equally refreshing was Ed's professional attitude. He was serious about finishing his book. And he was determined to find it a publishing home.

I used what little experience I had as a working freelance writer to help answer his industry questions. But when my long foundering marriage finally gave up the ghost and my time-to-assignment ratio shifted substantially, my opportunity to chat vanished. So did my friendship with Ed. It's tough to sustain a relationship based on computer messaging alone when you can't computer message anymore. And I simply had no time for anything else.

A year or so later a note came to me from Ed's original publisher, along with a book in brown paper. "Ed asked me to send you a copy," he wrote. Turns out, at least one of the Balboa rumors was true. Ed did have staying power. He'd finished his book and here it was, securely in print, ISBN number and all.

A couple of years later, after I'd established myself as a salable writer and moved to Spokane, Washington, Ed saw a piece I'd written for Writer's Market. Since my email address was included at the close of the piece, Ed reached out to re-establish a connection. And we've been very close friends ever since.

Anyone that knows Ed, knows that he likes to call himself the "Forrest Gump of Literature," meaning he sort of stumbled into success with a cheerful heart and an empty, half-addled mind. But don't let his humor fool you. This man is a storyteller at heart. He didn't trip up and land in a publisher's lap. He carefully plotted his approach and landing - the same way he networked his way to this paperback deal.

So read "Sex, Dead Dogs, and Me" with an open mind and with BTO throbbing in the background. You're about to experience a slice of Georgian Americana as sweet and real as pecan pie with vanilla ice cream on top. The odds are quite good that you'll literally savor every bite....

Visit Ed's website at: http://www.ed-williams.com

Want to e-mail Ed? You can at: ed3@ed-williams.com